Clare

The killing of a gentle activist

CHRISTOPHER CLARK

Dear Ann,

I hope you find some meaning in Clare's story, as I have.
Happy reading.

TAFELBERG

Christopher

Tafelberg
An imprint of NB Publishers
A division of Media24 Boeke (Pty) Ltd
40 Heerengracht, Cape Town, 8000
www.tafelberg.com

Cover design by Wilna Combrinck
Book design by Marthie Steenkamp
Edited by Mike Nicol
Proofread by Sally Hofmeyr

All photographs © Stewart family collection and Francois du Toit

'In Detention' by Chris van Wyk, from *It is Time to Go Home*,
Ad Donker, 1979. © Kevin and Karl van Wyk.

'The child who was shot dead by soldiers in Nyanga' by Ingrid
Jonker, from *Ingrid Jonker, Black Butterflies, Selected Poems*,
translated by Andre Brink, 1988. © Human & Rousseau.

Set in Tex Gyre Pagella

First edition, first impression 2022

ISBN: 978-0-624-09280-3
Epub: 978-0-624-09281-0

Printed by **novus print**, a division of Novus Holdings

For Colette, whose future still lies ahead of her.

Foreword

Our beloved sister Clare was assassinated in late 1993 in rural KwaZulu, like so many other people during the brutal apartheid years. Back then, being part of the ANC in the struggle against oppression was an honour.

She was committed to justice and freedom for all South Africans and worked in community development and political activism in the rural areas. Clare spoke fluent Zulu, lived simply, was deeply engaged in her work and community and, ultimately, died for her convictions.

My sister paid a high price. But with the ANC currently riven by factions, it is easy to forget how vital and essential it was back then.

We were ordinary South Africans, but we were also hardly South African at all. Though we were both born in South Africa, we did not live here until much later, but when we did the country definitely became home. Clare's death, though, was a South African murder of the worst kind. What did her killing achieve, so close to the country's first democratic elections?

Clare came from a family that was normal in many respects but also very different from most white South African families. Her young life was spent in independent African countries, a far cry from the South Africa of the 1960s and 1970s, which was a period of repression that started with the Sharpeville massacre in 1960 and continued to the Soweto uprisings of 1976. At least we were socialised and politicised in places far from white South Africa.

We were always very close, she and I, not just because our birthdates were thirteen months apart, but also because of our peregrinations around the world. At the many different schools we attended, we were always in each other's company. At State House Girls High School in Nairobi, we were allowed to swim unsupervised in the school pool, as long as we were together. We swam before school, at break, at lunchtime and before going home. Later we both went to Our Lady of Wisdom Convent in Limbe, Malawi. I remember on the first day trying to roll up our skirts at the waistband to make them shorter because we weren't accustomed to the 'cover the knee' edict of Hastings Kamuzu Banda, Malawi's president at the time. In 1972 it was miniskirt and hotpants time, but not in Malawi.

Our parents' commitment to social justice and class and racial solidarity, which was profoundly influenced by their progressive Catholicism enlivened by Vatican II (which changed the structures and practices of the church), permeated our lives as we got older. And so did books and books and books, game parks and holidays, often at Catholic mission stations in remote beautiful spots in Kenya and Malawi.

Clare took on these values more than any of her siblings, and certainly with much less contradiction between her views and her lifestyle. After her O-levels in Malawi, which she completed the year before the family was deported from that country, she did voluntary work in the UK and the US.

Back in South Africa in 1978, Clare began her agricultural career and carried on with her political conscientisation. Our lives intersected again in Zimbabwe in the early 1980s. Those were exciting revolutionary times in the newly independent country.

Our sons were both born there and it was lovely to be mothers, working, looking after children, running households, singing together, talking and talking, exchanging books, living a completely normal life – that's what we all want, isn't it? The abnormality of apartheid South Africa was just over the horizon, though.

I would like to thank Christopher Clark for becoming interested in Clare and her story. His research and book have brought her back into focus, returning her to me so deeply.

I have reread her letters to me for the first time in two decades – the letters she sent from Manguzi to the UK, where I was studying. The mix of the endlessly concerned mother and the cattle project co-ordinator, the hopes for the future both for herself and her children and for South Africa. The difficulties of being an ANC activist in an area fraught with violently competing interests. The problems of no electricity, typhoid in the well, and a cobra in the rubbish dump. The sorrow of sending her son Themba away to boarding school as a six-year-old. The deep concern for me, far away at Oxford Brookes. 'Are you happy?' she kept asking me.

Thank you, Chris, for taking us, in September 2021, on that roundabout trip in KwaZulu-Natal to the places where Clare had lived and worked. It highlighted her life. She lived in the workers' houses, and not somewhere special because she was white; it showed the steady development of her work with cattle; she learnt to speak Zulu; she used minibus taxis to travel, only much later buying an old VW Beetle. The trip brought Clare back to her children, Puleng and Themba, in profound ways.

After Clare died, friends in Johannesburg rallied around me and the children and found us somewhere to live, and we ended up living next door to Lis Lange. Lis has been a central part of our lives since 1997, and later became my wife; we all owe her a debt of gratitude.

Clare's life and death should inspire new resolve and commitment to building social justice in South Africa.

I miss her so much. We miss her so much.

Rachel Stewart

Author's note

Memory is a fickle, malleable and often unreliable tool for journalists to work with, particularly when it concerns events that happened many years ago. However, in various sections of this book, the memory of Clare's colleagues, friends and family was my sole resource from which to reconstruct aspects of her life and trajectory.

In some cases, there were inconsistencies and discrepancies between different people's recollections. For clarity and ease of reading, I have generally tried to stick to the most widely held version of events throughout this book.

In other instances, I have sought to reconstruct in vivid detail how events unfolded, based on a wide range of archival material. But this, too, remains a subjective and at times flawed approach.

All of which is to say that, however thorough and extensive my research, any sections of this book that draw on the distant past are, ultimately, my own interpretation or imagining of the events described rather than the absolute truth, if such a thing even exists.

Cast of characters

The family

Clare Stewart
Jimmy Stewart, Clare's father
Joan Stewart, Clare's mother
John Stewart, Clare's brother
Peter Stewart, Clare's brother
Alice Stewart, Clare's sister
Rachel Stewart, Clare's sister
Themba Stewart, Clare's son
Puleng Lange Stewart, Clare's daughter
Anne Hope, Clare's aunt
Kathy Stewart, Clare's sister-in-law
Sipho Cele, Puleng's father
Mosted Venge, Themba's father
Thembalethu Cele, Puleng's half-brother
Sithembiso Cele, Puleng's half-brother

Clare's friends

Neil and Creina Alcock
Nora Seleka
Jane Quin
Vanda van Speyk
Steve Hulbert
Peter Rutsch
Francois du Toit

The cattle co-operative
Khotiza 'Mbekaphezulu' Ngubane, chairperson
Jabulani Tembe, administrator
Mandla Ntuli, driver and assistant

The Truth and Reconciliation Commission investigators
Gail Wannenburg
Erik Kjaergaard

Police officers
Detective Dlamini, Jozini South African Police Service (SAPS)
Lappies Labuschagne, Jozini Special Branch
Andre van der Westhuizen, Newcastle Murder and Robbery Unit
Captain Rassie Erasmus, Newcastle Murder and Robbery Unit

The African National Congress (ANC)
Mcabango Mthiyane
Ronnie Kasrils
Bill Anderson

Key suspects
'Julius'
Aubrey Mngadi, Jozini Special Branch and Vlakplaas
Captain Nel, Jozini Special Branch
Hazel Buthelezi
Isaac Ntsele, Inkatha Freedom Party (IFP)
Gideon Zulu, IFP

Other Manguzi residents

Makotikoti
Doreen Ngubane
Busisiwe Mngomezulu

Journalists and fixers

Sam Reinders
Zimbili Vilakazi
Nomfundo Xolo

Contents

The road to Ingwavuma

September 2018

It was a bitterly cold morning. My photographer friend Sam Reinders and I drained a quick coffee and set out from our guesthouse on the edge of Manguzi before dawn, hoping to catch the best of the morning light. We made our way inland from the KwaZulu-Natal coast, driving in silence through a series of dilapidated rural towns whose buildings were caked in fine red dust. Men in blue overalls and beanies streamed along the potholed pavements on their way to work.

As the road neared the town of Ingwavuma, beyond which lay the Eswatini border, it began to climb sharply into the rugged Lebombo Mountains, revealing views of a vast, open stretch of sandveld below us. It was an area that was aptly known to the Zulus as 'uMhlabuyalingana' – 'the great flat place'.

After meandering up the mountainside for a couple of kilometres, we parked our rental car on a patch of gravel at the edge of the road and clambered out into a stiff breeze which carried the faint sound of a church choir incanting a melancholic harmony somewhere nearby.

'She must have been around here,' I said, vaguely gesturing at our rocky surroundings as I double-checked the GPS co-ordinates

I'd saved on my phone. Sam wandered away from the road, snapping photos. I jotted down a few notes describing the scene, then tried to imagine what it might have looked like twenty-five years ago, when Clare Stewart's decomposing body was finally found, a few metres from this stretch of road in a shallow ditch, presided over by a cluster of tall red aloes.

These days, it would be hard to get away with such a callous and brazen execution and disposal of a corpse here. The once remote dirt road had long since become a busy, tarred thoroughfare; cars and trucks hurtled past us as we snooped around. A number of small, low-slung breezeblock houses were dotted across the parched hillside, some emitting thin plumes of smoke from cooking fires. I wondered whether any of the current residents had any knowledge of the heinous crime that had been committed in their backyard all those years ago, at that pivotal moment in South Africa's history, as the country precariously straddled the pre- and post-apartheid eras and the province teetered on the edge of civil war. So much of the violence that had beset KwaZulu-Natal during that time had since been swept under the carpet, so many families left without any kind of justice or even recognition of their loss. Clare's story was but one of many casualties of the country's 'new dawn', relegated to the margins of history as a carefully curated narrative of reconciliation gradually took hold.

For my part, I had come across Clare's story by chance through my wife's parents, whose lives had overlapped with Clare's for a time. I'd since begun to tentatively get to know Clare's now-adult children, Themba and Puleng. But they'd been too young when their mother was killed to remember anything much about her.

I'd also garnered little of substance from the cold, detached language of police reports and a brief Truth and Reconciliation Commission (TRC) investigation. Overall, my sense of Clare's

16

remarkable life and premature death was limited to the broadest of brushstrokes.

As such, I'd made the journey to Manguzi and its striking surrounds, where Clare had spent her final years, somewhat speculatively. Sam and I had just wrapped up a project about land activists in Durban and were a tantalising few hours' drive away. I'd decided to push my return flight to Cape Town back by a couple of days and head north. After some gentle persuasion, Sam, ever an amenable travelling companion, had agreed to join me, and we set off without any real expectations.

But as I stood in the place where Clare had most likely drawn her last breath, my burgeoning interest in her forgotten story hardened into conviction: I would try to get to the bottom of it all. Against a backdrop of renewed political tumult in KwaZulu-Natal, epidemic levels of violence against women nationally, and widespread disillusionment with the post-apartheid project, I felt that a space should finally be carved out for Clare in South Africa's increasingly contested sense of self.

Over the following three years, the different threads of her story would continue to consume me, coinciding with a period of change in my own life, and eventually resulting in this book. Along the way, I would be forced to confront many of my entrenched ideas about South Africa and its history, as well as face a number of my deepest fears and doubts. Ultimately, I would be left with as many questions as answers.

But that would all come later. Back on the roadside on that cold morning, Sam inevitably soon ran out of creative ways to photograph a place that, after all, bore no visible remnants of the brief moment of violence that had brought us there. We climbed into the car and headed back down the hill towards the coast. The sun had risen quickly into a cloudless blue sky. It was going to be a beautiful day.

PART ONE

A life

CHAPTER 1

Missing

Clare Stewart rose early as usual on the morning she disappeared. It was 10 November 1993, late spring in sultry northern KwaZulu. Warm sunlight streamed through the small windows of her two-room thatched homestead, which perched on a verdant hillside on the outskirts of the rural town of Manguzi, about 15 km south of the Mozambican border.

Clare wandered down to the well at the bottom of the grassy bank in front of her stoep and drew a couple of buckets of water by hand. She watered the small, flourishing rose garden and a few neat rows of sunflowers that she'd planted beside the house. It had always given her great satisfaction to watch things grow. Then she washed herself from a blackened cooking pot in an old zinc basin.

Back in her bedroom, where scorpions occasionally fell from the ceiling onto her thin mattress, she dressed in a loose khaki blouse, a floral-print dress and cheap plastic sandals. She perfunctorily tidied her tousled brown hair, which framed kind hazel eyes and an assertive jaw. An intrepid and experienced rural development worker, Clare had just turned thirty-four and was a single mother of two young children. She had moved to Manguzi about five years previously, joining a handful of progressive whites in this fraught and chronically underdeveloped corner of the KwaZulu homeland.

Her aim was to create a cattle co-operative and breed a strong Nguni stud herd to reinvigorate impoverished cattle populations and enable local black farmers to control the lucrative sale of bulls. Nguni cattle, revered by the Zulus for their hardiness, a prerequisite for survival in the region, had recently been registered as a distinct breed, considerably increasing the viability of the co-operative.

Clare had settled quickly in her new home, which had originally been built as a temporary camp for agricultural researchers from the University of Zululand, and which suited her principled frugality. She promptly set about the painstaking process of obtaining the various permissions required and securing a plot of land for her project from the local traditional authorities and communities.

With their buy-in, she erected fences and put in infrastructure for irrigation. She had also created a close-knit committee which she then took all over the province to meet successful Nguni cattle farmers. Perhaps most importantly, Clare carefully cultivated a sense among the co-operative's members that it really *belonged to them*, a still-revolutionary achievement in those days.

At the time of her disappearance, Clare was living alone with her 16-month-old daughter Puleng – 'blessing of rain' in Sotho. Puleng had been born towards the end of the previous year's drought, one of the worst in the province's recent history, when the well had nearly run dry and Clare had caught typhoid as a result.

With her work consuming much of her time and a dearth of good English-medium schools in the area, Clare had sent her eight-year-old son Themba away to boarding school two years previously, at King's Primary in the midlands, one of the first non-racial schools in the province. The separation was profoundly difficult for them both. Although Clare tried to visit Themba every second weekend, it was a gruelling 1 200 km round trip, and she was provisionally planning to move away from Manguzi to be closer to him.

But there were shadowy figures closing in around her who harboured other ideas.

At about quarter past seven that morning, Clare left Puleng in the care of her domestic worker, a thirty-six-year-old woman named Busisiwe Mngomezulu. She climbed into the co-operative's white Toyota bakkie and set off down the rutted dirt road that snaked away from the homestead towards town. She planned to stop at the small office she rented next to Manguzi's central hospital for a couple of hours before attending a meeting with two local Department of Agriculture officials to discuss the classification of Nguni cows within the co-operative.

A moment later, Mngomezulu heard the vehicle come to a stop and there were two sharp blasts of its hooter, which she initially took to mean that Clare had forgotten something and was trying to get her attention. But before she could venture outside to check, she heard the bakkie moving off again and, assuming that it had been a false alarm, continued with her work. Mngomezulu finished up at around four-thirty that afternoon, as brooding storm clouds rolled in from the coast. There was no sign of Clare, but Mngomezulu thought little of it – Clare was often late back from work. So she wrapped Puleng in a towel and strapped her to her back, then walked down the hill to her own nearby kraal, sure that Clare would be home soon.

Even as dusk descended, there was probably little reason for Mngomezulu to suspect anything untoward, or more precisely, that a nebulous plot against Clare had been forming for some time and had finally been carried out.

In a province that was increasingly violently divided between supporters of the African National Congress (ANC) liberation movement and the Zulu nationalist Inkatha Freedom Party (IFP), the latter often backed by the state security apparatus and white right-wing groups, Clare's immediate community mostly perceived her as apolitical. She was at particular pains to keep politics out of the co-operative, where, against the odds, she had brought together members from both sides of the fractious political spectrum.

Despite this, Clare was, in fact, an active and ardent ANC member. In 1987, she had been recruited into the party's armed wing, Umkhonto we Sizwe (MK), by its charismatic commander Ronnie Kasrils, whom she'd met after a Paul Simon concert in the Zimbabwean capital, Harare. Her older sister, Rachel, who was living in Zimbabwe, was dating another MK commander, who had made the introduction after many months of being pestered by Clare.

Clare was given some basic training and instructions to carry out reconnaissance work upon her return to South Africa, including surveillance of key routes in and out of the country. This she allegedly continued doing when she moved to Manguzi about two years later.

As political violence between the ANC and the IFP escalated across KwaZulu and wider Natal, leaving more than four thousand dead over the next few years, Clare's family worried that she was in an increasingly precarious position. A week before her disappearance, as many as five thousand young IFP loyalists had attended paramilitary training camps just a couple of hundred kilometres south of Manguzi, at the so-called Mlaba Camp.

The camp was run by IFP strongman Philip Powell, a former apartheid secret police officer, notorious gunrunner, and avid collector of Nazi memorabilia. When Mlaba was later raided by the authorities in April 1994, Powell was arrested with two boxes of ammunition, a Ruger semi-automatic firearm, a 9 mm pistol and a homemade shotgun in his personal possession.

Clare was certainly not oblivious to the potential risks of her politics, or her life choices. In the late 1970s, she spent almost two years living and working with Neil and Creina Alcock at their agricultural project in Msinga, the first of its kind in the country. As recounted by author Rian Malan in his often lurid *My Traitor's Heart*, Mdukatshani, as the Alcocks' venture was known, had become a 'place of pilgrimage' for many progressive young white people. By that stage, the Alcocks had already spent the best part of two decades 'living among Africans, like Africans,' as Malan put it, in the hope that one day they would create a 'kind of Eden' in rural KwaZulu. It was a vision that had a significant impact on Clare.

But in 1983, Neil was ambushed and shot through the neck while driving back from a peace meeting he'd arranged between warring local Zulu factions. When police arrived at the scene, Malan wrote, Neil Alcock was found 'lying on his face in the dust of Africa, dead.'

Clare was also close friends with a woman called Jane Quin, whose sister Jackie had been killed in exile in Lesotho in 1985, in what came to be known as the 'Maseru Raid'. Jackie's husband, an MK operative by the name of Leon Meyer, and four other MK members and three Lesotho nationals, were all killed in the attack by a police hit squad under the orders of infamous apartheid assassin Eugene de Kock.

The celebrated anthropologist and anti-apartheid activist David Webster was another of Clare's friends to meet a violent end. He was shot dead outside his home in Johannesburg in 1989, allegedly for uncovering evidence of the apartheid government's involvement in illegal ivory and rhino horn trading not far from Manguzi.

There were other friends and acquaintances, too, who had endured police harassment. And although the vast majority of the victims of political violence in KwaZulu and Natal were black, the relative immunity that Clare and other white leftists might once have felt was no longer a given.

Clare certainly went further than most in her attempts to integrate, helped by a good command of Zulu. But it was inevitable that she would become a conspicuous presence in the wider area. In fact, she immediately attracted attention, and a certain amount of ire, as a single white mother of two mixed-race children. She was also the only white to attend the launch of the ANC's branch in the town of Empangeni a little further down the coast in 1990. Later that same year, she organised for an ANC-supporting black lawyer to defend members of an ANC youth group from the local high school in Manguzi. They were accused of a brutal 'witch killing' as a wave of similar attacks swept across the region.

At the behest of Gideon Zulu, a firebrand local IFP leader and senior member of the Zulu royal family, some of the party's members had recently withdrawn their cattle from Clare's co-operative in protest against what Zulu perceived as her increasingly clear ANC allegiance. There were also murmurings of mysterious newcomers with 'foreign accents' asking questions about Clare around town, and even of an aborted abduction attempt.

With all this in mind, when Rachel came to stay with Clare for a few weeks in August 1992, Clare made her promise that should anything happen to her, Rachel would take care of Themba and Puleng. It was not a frivolous pact – both sisters realised it could become a reality, much as they hoped otherwise.

About six hours after Clare left home on 10 November, a dutiful traffic officer by the name of Frans Gunter was called to the scene of a crash in Empangeni. The town had become a particularly violent flashpoint in recent clashes between the IFP and the ANC, while allegations of murderous misconduct by the KwaZulu police, especially against ANC supporters, were also rife.

Gunter quickly understood that a young man driving a white Toyota bakkie had crashed into a Telkom vehicle at a busy downtown intersection. The driver, who Gunter later described as 'well-built with *kroes* hair', told the officer that the vehicle belonged to his father. But Gunter suspected that he was driving without a licence and told him to slide over to the passenger seat so that he could move the bakkie out of the road. As Gunter climbed into the driver's seat, the man opened the passenger door and fled. Gunter briefly gave chase, but the man disappeared into the crowd.

Still assuming he was only dealing with a minor traffic offense, Gunter let him go and began to inspect the car. When he slid the front seats forward, he found an AK-47 and a magazine containing twelve rounds hidden behind them. There was also a khaki blouse, a black bag full of dog-eared school textbooks and a crumpled cigarette butt on the floor in the front.

Gunter was joined at the scene by another officer named Christiaan Nel, who then drove the abandoned vehicle to Empangeni's central police station, a typically dour and otherwise nondescript red brick building just a short distance away. Here he noted down the registration number and opened a case file.

According to the subsequent South African Police (SAP) investigation diary, by the end of the following day, police had discovered that the car belonged to an Nguni cattle project in Manguzi and had been routinely driven by 'a Clare Veronica Stewart'. After initial questioning by police, 'it was found that Ms Stewart was due to meet with two members of the Department of Agriculture in Manguzi,' but had not turned up for the meeting. The two officials had subsequently gone to look for Clare at her office and at her homestead, but to no avail.

'So far, there has been no information in regards to her movements,' the day's diary entry went on. Then it proffered a chilling conclusion: 'It is assumed that she has been murdered'.

CHAPTER 2

Her own way

Though Clare always considered herself South African, most of her formative years were characterised by translocation, the backdrop to her young life populated by a steady procession of 'elsewheres'. Born in Johannesburg on 2 October 1959, by the time she arrived in Manguzi, in addition to South Africa, she had also lived for varying lengths of time in Lesotho, Malawi, Kenya, Zimbabwe, the United States, the United Kingdom, and Ireland.

This remarkably itinerant lifestyle was mostly a consequence of the progressive politics and radical Catholicism of her parents, Jimmy and Joan Stewart, which were firmly underpinned by strong social justice principles. An erudite and extroverted polymath, Jimmy was born into a petit bourgeois Cape Town family in 1922. After taking up a law degree at the University of Cape Town in the late 1930s at just sixteen years old, he began to develop a strong radical streak and soon became a fervent Trotskyist. He promptly joined a number of non-racial religious and political student groups that stood against the hardening segregationist stance of Jan Smuts' Union Party, which governed between 1938 and 1948.

After graduating, Jimmy continued to be heavily involved in emerging leftist political and rural movements. A presbyterian by upbringing, it was during this period that he converted to Catholicism, certain strands of which had espoused newly progressive ideologies during the Second World War. It was through Catholic

28

circles in the late 1940s that Jimmy met Joan, a shy but strong-willed young woman with a sharp intellect who was studying medicine at the University of the Witwatersrand in Johannesburg.

Joan's well-to-do British mother (her father had died in Italy during the war) did not see Jimmy as an appropriate suitor for her daughter due to his lower-middle-class background and his politics. Once Joan, who was ten years Jimmy's junior, had finished her degree (she switched from medicine to medical science), she was shipped off to Oxford in the UK to live with relatives and, ostensibly at least, move on from the relationship.

But the irrepressible Jimmy nimbly followed her, changed academic tack and took up a master's degree in English literature at Cambridge. The couple wed soon afterwards, in 1952. Joan's mother acquiesced to the union, though she did not attend the wedding, which was held in an imposing Neo-Romanesque Catholic church in the Oxford suburb of Headington. The couple then headed back to Cambridge together, where they rented rooms from the widow of renowned British writer GK Chesterton. In 1954, the couple's first son, John, was born in the small town of St Neots, outside Cambridge.

As Jimmy and Joan set about building their bright new life together, South Africa descended ever further into the moral abyss. The racist National Party government had assumed power in 1948, and two years later had implemented the draconian Group Areas Act, which tore the country apart and came to form the cornerstone of its apartheid policy.

Jimmy and Joan were both adamant that they did not want to raise children in such a place, choosing instead a semi-nomadic life of self-imposed exile. Apart from occasional brief holidays to see Jimmy's family in Cape Town or short hospital stays in Johannesburg for Joan to give birth while the couple were living in neighbouring Basutoland (now Lesotho) in the late 1950s and early 1960s, they would never return to South Africa.

Their second son, Peter, was born in 1956, their first daughter, Rachel, in 1958, followed by Clare 13 months later. All three were born in Johannesburg's Marymount Hospital. Their first childhood home was a modest stone staff house on the Roma campus of what is now the National University of Lesotho. At this university Jimmy had established the English department, where he then lectured. The children grew up speaking Sotho and English almost interchangeably.

In late 1962, the family moved to Cambridge, Massachusetts, after Jimmy had been awarded an Oppenheimer scholarship to pursue his doctorate in literature at Harvard. Here, Joan gave birth to the couple's fifth child, Alice, in 1963, the year that US President John F Kennedy was assassinated.

Jimmy eventually completed his PhD at Cambridge University in the UK in the mid 1960s. His specialisation was the modernist English writer and poet DH Lawrence, whose work frequently grappled with the dehumanising effects of modernity and industrialisation. Throughout most of the late 1960s and early 1970s, Jimmy held academic posts at universities, first in Kenya, then Malawi, then later in the US. His years away from South Africa did not dim his radicalism. In 1975, he and his family were deported from Malawi after he supported a Malawian colleague detained by the country's increasingly authoritarian president, Hastings Banda, and fell out with the government censor over the state's banning of certain texts from the university curriculum.

As Jimmy and Joan moved their family around the globe, they sent the children to a series of racially integrated or, in the case of Kenya and Malawi, overwhelmingly black schools. This was certainly an exceptionally unusual experience for white South Africans at the time, and it seemed a wholly conscious bit of social engineering on the part of the two young parents. Part of their primary initial motivation, after all, was to avoid sending their children to whites-only schools in South Africa. However, the near-constant movement and flux had negative consequences, too. Joan, who did a master's in theology at Notre Dame University in the US and also lectured, in addition to being the children's primary caregiver, became prone to bouts of depression and strong feelings of instability. These became particularly acute after the family's sudden ejection from Malawi.

The children, meanwhile, were always the new students in class, wherever they went. As a result, they often struggled to maintain deep and lasting friendships. But this also brought Clare and her siblings, as well as the family as a whole, closer together, which would ultimately make the impending tragedy that much harder to bear.

By the time she reached her teens, it was clear that Clare had inherited her parents' political views and commitment to social justice, not to mention their well-known stubbornness.

While living in the UK in the mid 1970s, after the family's deportation from Malawi, Clare did a stint as a volunteer in a multiple sclerosis centre in Wales; looked after the aged at a care home; and volunteered for Meals on Wheels in Cambridge. Throughout, she insisted on wearing sandals, even in the depths of winter. In New York soon afterwards, and barely out of high school, she joined the *Catholic Worker*, a radical activist newspaper, where she penned occasional articles in addition to willingly carrying out a range of more menial tasks.

Clare's unusual upbringing continued to inform her decisions when she finally returned to South Africa from the UK, joining

Rachel in Lisbon with two budget plane tickets to Johannesburg in September 1978. The sisters were both on the cusp of their twenties, yet until then, the country of their birth had remained little more than an abstraction, an almost mythical land of freedom fighters and wild frontiers. As they entered adulthood, Clare and Rachel both felt a growing desire to better understand their proverbial native land and to feel a greater proximity to its righteous struggle.

Soon after arriving, Rachel met and fell in love with a so-called coloured man, with whom she moved to Zimbabwe in 1980. The couple sought to escape South Africa's Immorality Act, which prohibited, among other things, sexual relations between white people and other races, and to be part of Zimbabwe's independence movement.

Clare, meanwhile, had spent most of 1979 living and working with the Alcocks at Mdukatshani after she and Rachel had first visited the project together in late 1978. But ever restless, she relocated to Durban not long before Rachel left for Zimbabwe. There, she eventually moved into a small flat with a friend of a friend called Nora Seleka. As she settled into her new home, Clare hung a framed, hand-painted leaf on the wall in the hallway inscribed with an excerpt from the gospels. It read: 'Unless a seed falls to the earth and dies, it cannot bear fruit'.

Clare got a job at a local independent bookshop and immersed herself in books about popular peasant movements in Latin America and China. Part of her job was to send academic textbooks to political prisoners on Robben Island. She would occasionally sneak more politically incendiary reading materials into the packages. Through this small act of protest and the secret that she came to share with the prisoners, she felt a little closer to them and to their cause. She also worked at a cake shop, which provided sustenance of a different sort.

Clare's leftist politics were combined with an innate openness that also brought her into more direct contact with a number of young black South Africans who formed part of the growing resistance to apartheid. It was just a few years since the bloody Soweto Uprising, and the racist state-sanctioned violence and political repression were nearing their zenith. But it was also a heady and hedonistic time of jazz and clandestine township jols. After all her years abroad, Clare's passion was fuelled by her exposure to all the different kinds of South Africans calling for change.

Many of her new friends and acquaintances would frequently end up crashing on the couch in her and Nora's flat after long nights spent setting the world to rights. One such figure was a charismatic and quick-witted young trade unionist and ANC activist called Sipho Cele, who knew Nora through Catholic youth groups.

Perpetually curious, Clare once managed to convince Nora that the two of them should visit Sipho at his home in the township of Chesterville. They took a blacks-only bus across town and ended up sleeping in armchairs in Sipho's lounge, having missed the last bus back. Years later, the budding friendship between Sipho and Clare would come to have a profound and lasting impact on both of their lives and legacies.

For now, Clare was still busy trying to find her own path. In 1981, she left Durban and spent a year working on a sugarcane farm in the rural Natal town of Melmoth. She refused the invitation of the white farm owner, a family acquaintance called Robin van der Plank, to stay in the main farmhouse, requesting instead to lodge in the same basic cottages as the black farmworkers and insisting on receiving the same meagre pay. It was an experience that broadened her understanding of the poverty that plagued the rural areas. It was also here that Clare learnt to drive a bakkie, to make a fire, and to understand some basic Zulu.

It wasn't long before she developed a reputation on the farm as a bit of a rabble-rouser. On one occasion, van der Plank was warned by some of his senior farm employees that Clare was planning to organise a workers' strike. On another, he had to bail her out of the local jail after she was arrested for visiting a fellow farmworker's home in Melmoth's township.

The arrest put Clare on the radar of the local security police, who promptly called van der Plank into a back room of a featureless building in the centre of town and asked him to keep an eye on her. Clare, however, seemed undeterred by the whole affair, and continued to attend political and trade union meetings.

But despite her political and ideological conviction, Clare could be burdened by crippling self-doubt and diffidence and, like her mother, was sometimes prone to depression. She often struggled to make important decisions or put up appropriate boundaries. As a result, her life occasionally seemed to unfold as if it were not in her own hands. She was also plagued by the nagging sense that she was an outsider wherever she went. She yearned to belong somewhere and to have a clear sense of purpose. She abhorred so much of what she witnessed in white South Africa, yet she still felt removed from the plight of the marginalised black majority. Clare increasingly came to see the nascent sector of rural development as a potential means of bridging this gap.

With this new path in mind, after Melmoth, Clare attended the Chibero College of Agriculture in rural Zimbabwe, where she won the award for best agricultural-engineering student in 1984. She also met a handsome and charming Zimbabwean fellow student called Mosted Venge. They would study together in the library and Venge would patiently explain Zimbabwean politics to her.

The pair soon became intimate, and a few months later Clare was pregnant. The relationship didn't last, however. Venge's family convinced him that, although they had grown fond of Clare, the cultural chasm between them was too great. Innately forgiving, Clare harboured no hard feelings after the split, and prepared to raise her baby without a father.

While Clare was at Chibero, her parents were back in Maseru, where, in 1978, they'd started a joint project called Transformation of Southern Africa in the Light of the Gospels. Founded on the principles of non-racialism and liberation theology, the centre hosted seminars and meetings with political and religious activists and radical luminaries from all over the globe. True to its name, it became a prominent beacon of light, while South Africa remained in the shadow of apartheid, just over the Lesotho border.

When Jimmy wasn't otherwise occupied at the centre, he continued to give occasional guest lectures at the National University of Lesotho in the striking Roma Valley about 35 km south of Maseru. On 11 July 1984, he was driving to Roma from Maseru in the afternoon with Joan when a drunk Tanzanian professor from the university crashed into their car. Joan and the professor were both killed instantly. A badly injured Jimmy slipped into a coma and died three days later in hospital.

Clare was writing her final exams at Chibero at the time, and her siblings decided to wait for a few days before breaking the news to her. She had only told her parents about her pregnancy a few weeks before the accident, and had split from Venge just a couple of weeks before that. Much too soon, she now had to make her own way without parental support.

At least the siblings still had each other. After Clare graduated, she got a job at the Matopos Research Station, an agricultural project near Bulawayo, Zimbabwe's second-largest city. Rachel was living in Bulawayo and working as a journalist at a local English-language newspaper. After almost six years spent mostly apart, the two sisters became closer than ever. Rachel was at Clare's bedside when Themba ('hope' in Zulu and the Zimbabwean language Ndebele) was born on 17 January 1985.

Clare's oldest brother, John, was also living in Harare, with his wife, Kathy, who was Creina Alcock's sister. Kathy had been staying at Mdukatshani during Clare's time there and had met and fallen for John when he came to visit his sister. John, who'd been heavily involved in the Catholic Commission for Justice and Peace in Zimbabwe immediately after the country's independence in 1980, was now teaching science at a local Catholic high school in the country's capital.

Clare and Rachel would regularly take the overnight train from Bulawayo to visit their brother and see other friends, always booking a private two-berth coupé as a little luxury. Clare would bring her guitar and the two sisters would pass the time singing songs by the famous Chilean folk singer and communist activist Víctor Jara, who'd been tortured and killed in the first days of the bloodthirsty dictatorship of Augusto Pinochet. Despite the recent loss of their parents, these were happy times for both sisters, imbued with the youthful optimism of a newly liberated country. But further tragedy awaited.

In 1987, Rachel moved back to Harare and Clare returned to South Africa to take up a position as an agricultural assistant managing the dairy herd of a worker-managed co-operative farm in Bethlehem in the Orange Free State. It was an election year, and the climate in South Africa was particularly tense. The government of President PW Botha had recently imposed a repressive state of emergency in an attempt to stamp out the increasing internal opposition to apartheid.

Meanwhile, the state's growing proclivity for violence had prompted belated widespread international condemnation and exclusion. This did not stop a string of high-profile political assassinations at home and in neighbouring countries, including Swaziland (now Eswatini). In response, MK's violent resistance also ramped up, culminating in a number of fatal bomb attacks in urban centres. It was on a return trip to visit Rachel in Harare during this fraught period that Clare was introduced to Ronnie Kasrils and recruited into the ANC's armed wing.

But when she was in the Orange Free State, Clare was in the ancestral heartland of the Afrikaners, far from the progressive circles she had grown used to. In recent years, the province had become a hotbed of activity of Eugène Terre'Blanche's white-supremacist, neo-Nazi, paramilitary organisation, the Afrikaner Weerstandsbeweging, commonly known by its abbreviation, AWB. Among other things, the AWB wanted to re-establish the independent Boer Republics, including the Republic of the Orange Free State.

As Clare travelled around some of the province's backwater towns with the young Themba, the flagrant racism and constant shunning they encountered gradually began to wear her down. It became increasingly clear that she wasn't going to find the sense of belonging she sought in the Orange Free State.

So it was that when an old acquaintance and fellow rural development worker, Steve Hulbert, invited her to KwaZulu to help set up a new community-based Nguni cattle project, she jumped at the opportunity.

CHAPTER 3

An opportunity

Just a few kilometres inland from the coastal lake ecosystems of Kosi Bay, Manguzi had been known by many names during the preceding century, each of them speaking to some part of its colourful and contested history. The name Manguzi itself was believed to stem from the abundance of wild mango trees in the area. Among other landmarks, this name was also applied to the local hospital, built by the Methodist church in the 1940s, about twenty-five years after the church had founded a small mission in the area.

Many locals, however, still knew the town and its surrounds as KwaNgwanase after the Mabudu-Tembe king who'd ruled from the late nineteenth to the early twentieth century. During that time, it had been more widely known as Tembeland or Thongaland.

By the latter part of the nineteenth century, the colonial powers of Britain and Portugal and the South African Republic had all laid claim to the wider region, which was often referred to as Maputaland (a slight distortion of Mabudu-land). In 1875, the French president, Patrice de MacMahon, had arbitrated in the matter and a line was drawn that would cleave the Mabudu chiefdom in two and constitute the South Africa–Mozambique border. In 1897, almost twenty years after the bloody Anglo-Zulu War, Britain formally annexed the area that now comprises Kosi Bay to its Natal colony.

Until the 1960s, the South African government recognised the people of Maputaland as ethnically Thonga. Then, in 1976, Maputaland was incorporated into the KwaZulu homeland (which MK combatant and historian, Visit Zulu, labelled a 'puppet creation' of apartheid) and its people were reclassified as Zulu.

In 1982, contestation over the region surfaced again when it emerged that the government intended to cede Maputaland to neighbouring Swaziland, a move that was supported by certain prominent Mabudu-Tembe chiefs, but fiercely challenged by KwaZulu Prime Minister Mangosuthu Buthelezi. However, when Clare arrived in Manguzi in 1989, it was a tranquil and laid-back place where many of the inhabitants still gained their livelihoods from the abundant resources of the lake. While the men fished with the same cleverly designed wooden traps they had used for centuries, the women harvested inter-tidal resources such as mussels, chitons, sea cucumbers, octopi and crabs.

When she first arrived in town, Clare stayed with Steve Hulbert and his wife Vanda in their modest bungalow, which sat among a dozen or so such properties on a scrubby but well-shaded plot of land beside Manguzi Hospital. The plot was dotted with a number of wild mango trees. This was effectively the heart of Manguzi's small white community, which consisted of a handful of hospital staff, a couple of teachers from the Star of the Sea Catholic mission school, a few rural development workers from the University of Zululand, and the owner of the local Spar and his wife.

Working closely with traditional leaders, Steve and a fellow member of the local University of Zululand unit, Charles Louw, had recently set up a farmers' co-operative called Thuthukani ('to develop' or 'to improve' in Zulu) to help black farmers pool their resources. The co-op consisted of a general dealer that sold everything from seed to cement as well as produce from a community garden at Thandizwe. Members could buy wholesale and therefore get better prices. At its peak in the early 1990s, Thuthukani did about forty per cent of all co-op business in KwaZulu and Natal. Thuthukani was also installing ventilated improved pit latrines (known locally as VIPs) across the area.

Steve was thinking of adding a cattle co-operative, under the umbrella of Thuthukani, after observing both the integral role that Nguni cows played in Zulu culture and their largely untapped potential for economic upliftment. White farmers in outlying areas had cottoned on to the significant value of this particularly resilient and well-adapted cattle breed and were attending cattle auctions all over Maputaland, acquiring Nguni cattle, which were routinely undervalued by their black owners. Steve and Charles believed that a cattle co-operative could better empower local black farmers, capitalising on and further improving the existing value of the area's bovine bloodstock.

After their initial consultations with Clare, it was agreed that the creation of an Nguni stud herd would help provide sustenance (meat and milk) for communities where levels of child malnutrition were often high, as well as a co-ordinated commercial revenue stream. The new venture was dubbed the Masivela-kwaTembe Nguni Cattle Co-operative. 'Masivela' can be roughly translated as 'when we arise'.

Clare soon set up in an office on the Thuthukani premises. These comprised a small cluster of concrete buildings next to Manguzi Hospital. She threw herself into her new work quickly and with relish, excited by its potential and the feeling that she was at the forefront of building something from the ground up. Initially, many of the locals were mildly bemused by the sight of a young white woman doing 'men's work' such as dealing with cattle or putting up fences. But Clare's patience, humility and good command of Zulu soon won people over. After about a month at Steve and Vanda's house, she moved into the former temporary University of Zululand camp at Thandizwe.

She quickly developed a number of firm friendships among Manguzi's small white population, most of whom were relative newcomers with similarly adventurous spirits and progressive politics.

Themba also adapted to his new life with relative ease. The Sotho he had picked up on the farm in Bethlehem was promptly replaced by Zulu and he too made new friends at the local nursery school.

Clare had finally found the greater sense of belonging and purpose she had long sought. She was happy and at ease in herself. But the idyll would not last.

On New Year's Eve 1989, Clare and Themba arrived at Thandizwe in the late afternoon after a couple of weeks away. They had celebrated Christmas in Durban with Clare's brothers, Peter and John, then stopped in for a couple of days with an old friend of Clare's on their way back up the coast.

They'd enjoyed a good and welcome break, but Clare wanted to get back to Manguzi to attend a party at Steve and Vanda's house later that evening: 'Returning home to start the New Year with familiar friends,' as she wrote soon afterwards in a letter to her sister Rachel.

But Clare returned to find that her homestead had been broken into. 'As I unlocked the door, I saw the window was open,' she wrote. 'All my papers had been taken out of drawers and were upside down and other such obvious things. Nothing stolen though. It was all very suspicious.' It was the third time she had been broken into in the past few months.

Clare then drove to Steve and Vanda's house to find out what time the evening's festivities were to start. She also told them about the latest break-in but downplayed how unsettled it had left her feeling. 'I didn't want to arrive and see them for the first time in a while by bringing depressing news – some dependent character who needed to lean on others,' she wrote.

By the time Clare and Themba got back to Thandizwe again and finished unpacking from the trip, it was already dark. Clare lit a candle and was getting ready to leave for the party when she heard a loud rustling outside.

John had given her a powerful new torch for Christmas, which she used to scan the front of her house. The torch's cold light eventually caught a crouched figure pressed against the wall not far from the front door. He held what looked like a panga in one hand, and a knife glinted in the other.

'I don't know if I retreated or if he forced me back inside, or if he shouted, but I remember backing into the house and a roar of fear and shock coming out of me … and Themba standing next to me screaming, and three men/boys jumping into the house,' Clare wrote.

The oldest of the three was a heavy set man of about twenty, who had a shirt wrapped around his face; the youngest couldn't have been older than twelve. All three wielded pangas.

The intruders spoke to each other in a mix of Zulu and broken English, expressing angry disappointment at Clare's lack of valuable possessions as they turned the place upside down. Clare's legs buckled and she sat down on an armchair and held Themba close. She tried to tell him that the intruders just wanted money and would cause them no harm. But then the oldest of the group ran his hand up Clare's thigh and told her to go into the bedroom and lie down.

Two of the three raped her on her own bed. She kept a hand on Themba throughout. She had managed to cover him with a

42

blanket and pillows to spare him from seeing what was happening to her. Despite her own fear and the violence being inflicted upon her, she kept trying to reassure him. 'It's OK. It's OK. I'm here,' she said again and again as he screamed incessantly.

After the rapists were done, the oldest swaggered around, swigging from a bottle of wine and forcing Clare to do the same at knifepoint. He then looked at pictures on the wall and demanded that Clare tell him who was in them. The younger boy suddenly became aggressive and had to be restrained from attacking Clare with his panga.

Finally, they decided to leave. They blew out the candle, took the new torch, told Clare not to move, then locked the door from the outside before slinking away into the darkness.

Clare and Themba lay paralysed by fear. It was late, and Themba eventually fell into a fitful sleep. About half an hour later Clare heard a car approaching.

'I jumped out of the window, hurled myself down towards the road shouting and screaming and the car turned in towards the house, streaming amazing bright light,' she wrote to Rachel. 'Steve jumped out of the car and met me halfway and I collapsed into his arms, sobbing and saying, "I've been raped, I've been raped." Themba had woken up and also climbed onto the window ledge and was crying "Don't leave me!"'

When Clare hadn't arrived at the New Year's Eve party, the other guests had become worried and Steve drove to Thandizwe to check on her. He now drove them back to his and Vanda's house, then took Clare to Manguzi Hospital for one of the doctors, a friend of Clare's called Cally Todd, to examine her.

Although Clare was still frightened and in shock, Cally would later recount in a letter to Clare's aunt, Anne Hope, how 'she seemed amazingly strong through it all'.

Clare and Themba stayed with Steve and Vanda for the next couple of weeks. During this time, Clare was visited by senior police officers from Vryheid, but given the politics of the time, she was both suspicious of and felt judged by them. 'Bloody SAP,' she wrote in another letter to Rachel in late January 1990. Despite police attempts to reassure her, the rapists were never arrested, though their identity was widely known.

After her time at Steve and Vanda's, Clare stayed for another few weeks with her close friend Jane Quin in Durban, where she and Themba also both separately received trauma counselling. 'It was OK – helpful in a way I suppose, though not that different to talking to sympathetic friends,' Clare wrote of the experience.

Jane made a conscious effort to take Clare out and have as much fun as possible. Despite her recent ordeal, Clare was a willing participant, and the two women's time together was filled with laughter.

Clare would not let the rape deflect her and by February 1990 she and Themba were back in Manguzi. With the security situation across the province beginning to worsen, many of the other whites tried to convince Clare to move to one of the houses on the hospital grounds, but she was set on staying at Thandizwe. Her ideological conviction was unwavering, and she was deeply discomfited by the idea of affording herself any additional privileges or protection so long as they remained unattainable for the majority of South Africans.

Shortly after her return, on Sunday 11 February 1990, Clare and Themba joined a number of her friends as they gathered around the TV at Steve and Vanda's house to watch Nelson Mandela's long-awaited release after twenty-seven years in prison. There was an impromptu party to celebrate the historic moment. Clare and Themba stayed until late. In that moment, Clare was happy and filled with hope.

The cattle project continued to progress slowly but surely. Much of Clare's time in her first year in Manguzi was spent writing fundraising proposals and at long community meetings, where she was constantly aware of the area's entrenched age and gender divisions. By 1991, her patience and diligence with regard to both aspects were finally beginning to pay dividends. In addition, the co-operative had swelled to more than fifty members and Clare had successfully obtained a grant from a Dutch funding agency called Novib, which had a particular interest in rural development.

After a protracted period of sometimes-tense negotiations with traditional authorities, Clare and Khotiza Ngubane, a local traditional healer who had been elected as the cattle project's chairman, managed to obtain a 365-hectare plot from the KwaZulu Department of Agriculture and Forestry. The land was gradually fenced and a reservoir and windmill were put in to provide a consistent supply of water. Clare's male colleagues were impressed by her constant willingness to get her hands dirty.

During this time, Clare also reconnected with Sipho Cele, more than a decade after they'd first crossed paths in Durban. She and Sipho had initially kept in touch while Clare was working on the farm in Melmoth. He would let her know about political meetings in the area, where they would occasionally catch up when he was in attendance. This was followed by a period of silence while Clare was at agricultural college in Zimbabwe. Then, not long after she moved to Manguzi, they bumped into one another again at an ANC meeting in Empangeni, where Sipho was now living.

In the intervening years, Sipho had risen through the ranks of the growing trade union movement to become Northern Natal Regional Secretary for the Congress of South African Trade Unions (Cosatu). He had also become a prominent ANC organiser in

Empangeni and had secretly been sent to Lusaka in Zambia twice, to receive political and military training.

With Sipho's sharp sense of humour, mischievous smile and irrepressible charisma, politically inclined young men flocked to him. His small home became a kind of unofficial ANC youth centre. Clare would sometimes linger there after political meetings, always exhilarated to be in such company and equally allured by Sipho's magnetism. In turn, he occasionally stopped in to visit Clare at Thandizwe whenever he was working in the area. The two of them held long, passionate and frequently quarrelsome conversations about local politics and Zulu culture.

One evening in August 1991, Sipho and a few of his friends joined Clare for dinner at her home, where they discussed the negotiations at the Convention for a Democratic South Africa (Codesa) that were taking place in Johannesburg. As the night wore on, the other guests gradually departed, Themba was put to bed, and Sipho and Clare were eventually alone. Sipho was reluctant to drive back to Empangeni so late and asked if he could stay over. He and Clare slept together for the first time that night, and so began a sporadic romantic relationship.

Despite taking precautions, three months later, in November 1991, Clare was pregnant again. But she only broke the news to Sipho in February the following year, by which point their relationship was already fizzling out.

Among other things, Clare had grown concerned about Sipho's seemingly ever-worsening alcohol abuse. Also, his reluctance to talk to her about his estranged wife and his six children (who'd been born to three different women) began to drive a wedge between them. Sipho withdrew even further from Clare after she told him she was pregnant.

A month previously, Clare had also had to deal with the loneliness and rupture of sending Themba away to boarding school at

King's. It had become clear that Themba's pedagogical development was beginning to plateau at the local nursery school in
Manguzi, but there was also a dearth of nearby English-medium
alternatives where his individuality and budding creativity could
be sufficiently nurtured.

Initially, Clare had stayed with Sipho in Empangeni en route to
and from Nottingham Road to visit Themba on weekends. These
visits stopped abruptly after she disclosed her pregnancy. For
his part, Sipho was increasingly preoccupied with the mounting
violence between the ANC and the IFP in his township of Ngwelezane, where he feared his prominent ANC allegiance had put a
target on his back. Sure enough, on the afternoon of 14 March 1992,
a group of about a hundred IFP supporters descended on Sipho's
house. Some began to stone the property, while others opened
fire. Sipho escaped unharmed with the help of his neighbours,
but some of his fellow ANC supporters returned fire, and one of
the leaders of the IFP group was shot and killed.

At four-thirty the following morning, a group of men, their
faces covered, forced their way into Sipho's home and searched for
weapons, then proceeded to assault Sipho and a group of young
ANC activists who had stayed to protect him after the previous
day's attack.

Sipho and seventeen others were then taken to Ngwelezane
Police Station in unmarked vehicles, where their attackers continued
to assault them. Sipho suffered a broken nose, three fractured ribs
and a fractured ankle. He was sent to Empangeni Hospital for
treatment, where he spent the next three weeks. While he was away,
IFP supporters burned down his house.

Having belatedly heard about the attacks, Clare drove from
Manguzi to visit him in hospital. Though their romantic relationship was over, Sipho was moved by Clare's enduring concern

and her ability to put aside personal grievances. As they chatted, both were hopeful that their friendship would endure.

A couple of months later, in the early hours of the morning of 3 July 1992, Clare experienced severe labour pains at home in Thandizwe, and she was admitted to Manguzi Hospital a little after sunrise, where her friend Cally delivered a healthy baby girl. Cally would note in another letter to Clare's aunt Anne: 'Clare adored Puleng immediately and seemed to forget all the pain. She was instantly transformed.'

Ever robust, Clare was up and out of hospital the following day.

Manguzi, 22 June, 1993

Dear Anne,

Sorry for the red pen, but otherwise I won't write at all – and a letter to you is long, long overdue. I have just come back from work and Puleng is unusually asleep, so I have put on some supper and am taking these moments before she wakes.

Work was good today. We've divided the committee into three sub-committees: one to deal with the practical building of the project, one with training, and one with finances. So today we went out to plan with the practical group. It was very constructive, also exciting sitting down and planning what the project will look like – what options, where to build what ... I'm sorry to say we still haven't got cattle, but we haven't made any steps backwards this year, just slowly, slowly forward. July some cattle will be in, almost everything is ready for them. And next week we are interviewing some people for a trainee administrator/co-ordinator post, so responsibilities will be transferred to other people and I will be able to leave.

It's good this week is going well. Last week I had a disastrous committee meeting where I got cross and was rude to the chairman, who is usually so supportive of me. He got into an immense huff and left the meeting, refusing to accept an apology. I sat and cried and cried ... but somehow it was all weathered ... and we got through to another meeting. The day after tomorrow we go off on a work trip to Maritzburg, and also to pick up Themba for his July holiday, which will be great. I spend hours still wondering how to get Themba here – try to work part-time, 3/4 time and teach him from 7:30 to 10:30, and organise other activities for him?? It almost feels possible, and then I get scared that he will get lonely and bored here – and miss the camaraderie of school. (I phoned him last Saturday to say hullo, and he said school was fun. He and some friends were in the middle of making a fort in the woods and a pushcart and he was very excited about it all.)

I continue to miss him all the time. Themba more than anyone else in my life I miss when I am enjoying something ... like a party I went to the other evening – thinking if only Themba were here ... But as Puleng grows older they must be together more – she's growing into a determined kid, no longer a baby (except in her endless breastfeeding, and she's also pretty much a lost cause as [far as] sleeping at night is concerned).

It would of course be lovely if you could come here soon. Although things are finally taking shape, it does look as if I will still be here until late in the year, so plan your visit!

Life in Thandizwe is incomparably better this month because there are two students from Durban University doing community development diploma fieldwork – so almost for the first time since I have been here, there are people who feel like companions, who I find interesting to talk to and who I share meals with – my tension of being vulnerable and isolated is gone. But they leave in a couple of weeks. I am trying to organize that a woman who works in the Spar comes to stay with her two kids, which will be another kind of companionship, but probably of a less equal type.

Anyhow, since I started writing I stopped to play with Puleng, have supper with Mzizi and Zweli, talk, bath Puleng, put her to sleep, and now (at 9:15 pm) I should sleep so that I have enough hours' sleep, in-between waking for Puleng, by tomorrow morning.

Please write and let me know how you are and what your plans are.

Much love,

Clare

In August 1993, more than four years after Clare had moved to Manguzi, the cattle co-operative finally purchased its first carefully selected Nguni cows for their breeding herd. By October, they had twelve cows and a fine Nguni bull. In addition to providing both commercial value and a source of sustenance to the local community, the stud herd would also allow the co-operative to sustain itself without constantly needing to seek outside funding.

After countless community meetings and tireless campaigning by Clare and her executive, the co-operative also now boasted more than a hundred members. Miraculously, mutual respect and in some cases even friendships had flourished between co-op members of different political affiliations, even as political violence between the ANC and the IFP consumed more of the region daily.

Conscious of the growing security risk and still struggling to deal with Themba being at school so far away, not to mention exhausted by the gruelling 14-hour round trips to visit him on weekends, Clare told friends and family that she was planning to leave Manguzi. She felt that she had brought the project to a point where it could soon carry on successfully without her, and that her assistant and project administrator, Jabulani Tembe, was well equipped to take her place.

In the meantime, Clare did some tentative job-hunting. She planned to apply for a teaching position at Cedara College of Agriculture in Pietermaritzburg, just forty-five minutes away from King's and down the road from her close friend Jane Quin.

Clare's sister Rachel was also planning to return to South Africa from the UK. The sisters spoke about the possibility of living together. The country was changing, and suddenly they were both excited at the new opportunities they envisioned for themselves and their mixed-race children in a new country. (Rachel had also had a son in 1980.) For a moment, the future looked bright.

CHAPTER 4

Herders

By the time darkness fell on 10 November, the day of Clare's disappearance, her colleagues feared the worst. Jabulani Tembe drove to Thandizwe, where he tried to reassure Clare's domestic worker, Busisiwe, who was still looking after Puleng and beginning to worry. When he returned the next morning and there was still no sign of Clare, Busisiwe was distraught.

That same evening, Jabulani phoned Clare's brother Peter in Johannesburg to tell him the worrying news. Peter then told Rachel, who had arrived back in South Africa a few days previously, having finished her master's degree in business administration at Oxford Brookes University in the UK. She was staying with Peter and his wife while she considered her next move.

Meanwhile, one of Clare's friends from Manguzi Hospital, a visiting Irish doctor called Laura Campbell, had driven Puleng down to Jane Quin in Shongweni, about 40 km outside Durban.

The rest of the Stewarts converged on Jane's house on 13 November. Clare's bakkie had been found in Empangeni but there was no further news. Her brother John and his wife, Kathy, flew in from Harare. Her aunt Anne flew up from Cape Town. Once they were all assembled, Clare's siblings drove to Nottingham Road to deal with the unenviable task of having Themba summoned to the principal's office to tell him that his mother was missing and that they were going to pull him out of school.

As the news of Clare's disappearance spread, a steady stream of journalists descended on Jane's house to interview the family and take pictures of Clare's young children. 'We want our mom' was the headline above a picture of the two of them in one Sunday paper. In the photo, Themba wore a T-shirt that had the slogan 'no news is bad news' written across the front. It had been a gift from his uncle John on a previous visit and the slogan was a reference to the political struggle in Zimbabwe, but it suddenly took on a macabre new meaning with regard to Clare.

On 15 November, the family organised a press conference to further raise awareness, but after five days with no news, their sense of foreboding grew ever deeper.

Themba, meanwhile, became unusually quiet and withdrawn. However, as the older sibling, albeit only eight years old, he also seemed to take it upon himself to console Puleng. During this time, he was completely inseparable from his baby sister, who was not yet eighteen months old. Themba would frequently hold Puleng and whisper secret words of reassurance into her ear, perhaps as much for his own benefit as for hers.

Anne took it upon herself to keep close tabs on the initial police investigation. Clare's case had been assigned to a warrant officer from the Newcastle Murder and Robbery Unit called Andre van der Westhuizen. He told Anne that it was clear Clare was popular, as he had already received more than a hundred calls enquiring about her. Contrary to all the evidence at his disposal and his own initial conclusions, van der Westhuizen tried to reassure the family that he was confident Clare might still be found alive.

However, by 20 November, ten days after Clare had disappeared, with no new leads, the media lost interest in the story, as their attention returned to the ongoing Codesa negotiations and the hopeful prospect of a new South Africa.

Despondent and unsure what to do next, the family went back to their respective homes. There were long discussions about who would take Puleng and Themba, but given the pact she had made with Clare, Rachel was adamant that she should be the one to shoulder that responsibility. The children returned with her to Johannesburg, where a family friend offered to loan her a flat just a few blocks from Peter's house. Clare's younger sister, Alice, flew in from the US to stay with Rachel and the children just as John and Kathy flew back to Harare.

Creina Alcock, Kathy's sister, had also come down to Shongweni from Mdukatshani to see the family, and she had volunteered to drive the children through to Johannesburg as Rachel still didn't have a car. She ended up staying for a few days to lend a hand, cooking meals and helping with the children as Rachel tried to busy herself with job-hunting.

'There was a terrible emptiness, not knowing,' Creina wrote in a letter to another of Clare's friends shortly afterwards, 'and the Stewarts seemed almost catatonic in their responses, moving slowly, unhearing, as if spellbound.'

At about nine on the morning of 24 November 1993, two weeks after Clare went missing, in a valley below the gravel road from Manguzi to Ingwavuma, fourteen-year-old Mbuso Mngomezulu, his thirteen-year-old brother, Phiwayinkosi, and a neighbour called Bongani Mofuleka left their family compound and set out in search of their father's cattle. After about an hour, as they neared a dense clump of bushes where the cattle often grazed, just above the road, they came across a shallow ditch presided over by tall red aloes. Mbuso and Phiwayinkosi noticed a body lying face up with its wrists bound above its head with a leather belt.

Terrified, the boys turned and ran home and told their mother, Ngodomane Mngomezulu, what they had seen. By the early afternoon, she had organised a lift into Ingwavuma with a neighbour, where she took the boys to the police station to report the body and give statements.

'Although they said the body was decomposed, my children suspected that it was a female, since they noticed a dress,' Mngomezulu told the police when she gave her own statement.

Some hours later, a police sergeant by the name of Mphiwa Gina and a constable called Orthinial Nyawo drove the boys and their mother back to the scene, where the boys led them to the body hidden between the bushes. As the police officers made their initial inspection, it was clear that the body had been there for some time. Any remnants of skin that were still left on the mostly exposed skeleton had grown leathery and hard, while animals seemed to have gnawed at the bones, bleached a brilliant white by the sun.

The police officers noticed a small handbag still slung around the deceased's left arm. Sergeant Gina opened it and found an ID booklet inside. A photo of Clare stared back at him. As the two officers inspected the scene, they also found two spent and corroded AK-47 cartridges a few metres away from Clare's body.

The next morning, Clare's remains were retrieved from the scene and sent to Mosveld Hospital in Ingwavuma, where an initial autopsy noted 'fractures in facial bones, skull and cervical vertebra consistent with having been caused by a high-velocity bullet'. It was clear that Clare had been shot in the back of the head at close range.

Clare's skull was then removed and sent to the Durban Medico-Legal Mortuary, where the remains of her teeth and jaw were examined by a forensic odontologist. Compared with the records of Clare's private dentist, he concluded that the dental pattern showed a clear match.

The following day, van der Westhuizen added a curt closing entry to Clare's SAP investigation diary: 'Body is found'.

CHAPTER 5

Red flags

To Every Birth Its Blood, as the poet and writer Mongane Wally Serote had presciently observed in the title of his debut novel in 1981. Sure enough, as Clare's life was violently and prematurely curtailed, a brave new South Africa was on the cusp of being born. After more than two years of fraught negotiations at Johannesburg's World Trade Centre, in the early hours of 18 November 1993, eight days after Clare had disappeared, negotiators from across the country's political spectrum signed off on a progressive new interim constitution that would guarantee equal rights to all races. The passage of the 223-page document marked a pivotal turning point in the transition from apartheid to democracy.

Members of the ANC present in the capacious council chamber greeted the historic moment with cries of 'Amandla!' Conservative Party members of parliament, meanwhile, heckled the government benches and called President FW de Klerk a 'traitor', then rose to sing the apartheid national anthem 'Die Stem'.

'South Africa's main political antagonists this morning concluded their grand bargain to end white dominion,' read the *New York Times'* front-page story filed from Johannesburg that day, accompanied by a picture of a smiling Nelson Mandela shaking hands with de Klerk in front of their posse of negotiators.

Mandela issued a typically sunny statement from the ANC headquarters at Luthuli House, in Johannesburg, a little later that morning: 'Now, for the first time, the future holds the promise of a brighter tomorrow,' he said. Newspapers across the country heralded the dawn of a new era in a series of similarly optimistic headlines.

But in KwaZulu and Natal, the threat of civil war continued to loom large. IFP leader and ANC turncoat Mangosuthu Buthelezi was among a coalition of hard-line leaders who had boycotted the constitution-negotiation process. He maintained that his party would not take part in the forthcoming multiparty elections. Instead, he encouraged his party's supporters to actively disrupt them. As chief minister of the KwaZulu homeland, Buthelezi was largely driven by the fear that the ANC's plan to do away with divisive ethnic politics would erode his own hold on power and privilege in the region, which had depended to a large extent on the apartheid government's support.

There were at least two major IFP paramilitary training camps in the north of the homeland, and, during November 1993, the death toll from clashes between the ANC and IFP mounted into the hundreds. Nationally, the number of political killings was nearing three and a half thousand for the year, as the violence also spread to the hostels and townships of Johannesburg's East Rand, fuelled in part by the 'third force' destabilisation tactics of state security operatives.

Clare's family, who generally shared her progressive politics, were certainly well aware that her death was but one among many. 'In the last month, we have shared deeply in the anguish of so many families whose lives are disrupted by the violence sweeping the country,' wrote Anne Hope in a letter to friends and family in mid December.

Just a week earlier, the family had laid Clare to rest in the cemetery of the Marianhill Monastery, on the outskirts of Durban. A little more than forty years previously, her parents had got engaged there. In keeping with MK tradition, the hundred or so people assembled sang 'Hamba Kahle Mkhonto we Sizwe' ('Go Well Spear of the Nation) as the pallbearers, led by Clare's brothers Peter and John, lowered her simple coffin into the ground.

Five months later, on 27 April 1994, the country went to the polls in its first democratic elections. Black South Africans turned out in their millions to vote for the first time, standing for hours in snaking kilometre-long queues. The ANC was voted into power with more than 62.5 per cent of the vote.

But in early 1995, Mandela felt compelled to call for United Nations intervention in KwaZulu-Natal, which were formed into one province at the end of apartheid, as the IFP continued to clamour for greater autonomy from the ANC government. The army was also deployed to various provincial flashpoints to mitigate the violence. Amid the frenzied hope and violent chaos, the investigation of Clare's murder struggled to get off the ground. Police eventually identified the young suspect, said to be known by the nickname 'Julius', who had crashed the co-operative's Toyota bakkie and then fled the scene in Empangeni. Three witnesses, including a hitch-hiker, said they had seen Clare in the passenger seat beside this suspect on the morning of her disappearance. A couple of hours after those sightings, a petrol attendant saw Julius filling up Clare's bakkie at a petrol station in Ingwavuma. This witness said that Clare was nowhere to be seen. It was therefore assumed that she had been killed and disposed of somewhere in-between.

These were promising leads, but they came to nothing. Julius had apparently crossed the border into Swaziland after his close call in Empangeni, and he had since fallen off the police's radar. Other suspects also disappeared into thin air, including a 'strange black man', as a police witness statement put it, who was seen at Clare's gate by the eleven-year-old daughter of one of her neighbours shortly before Clare left home. The man allegedly introduced himself to the girl as Hazel Buthelezi and asked about Clare's car, which was parked outside her homestead. Like Julius, he vanished.

Ultimately, the investigation stalled without a single arrest. 'Although investigations are carried out thoroughly and impartially, this office is at this time in no position to speculate around the motive for the abduction and subsequent murder of the victim,' read a notably vague investigation report by van der Westhuizen during a brief inquest into Clare's murder in June 1995.

Meanwhile, various rumours did the rounds in Manguzi. Some locals thought that the hit had been a joint operation between the IFP and the Security Branch. There was some suggestion that Clare had still been in contact with ANC military intelligence in the area and that she had been involved in all manner of underground activities. Perhaps the cattle project was a front – a political Trojan Horse – all along, some wondered. Others pondered whether Clare's death wasn't an internal killing by the ANC.

In either instance, the assumed motive was that Clare must have come to know too much about something and needed to be silenced. Another local theory held that the whole thing was an inside job by members of the cattle project as they vied for power. Perhaps unsurprisingly for a small rural border town, there were also salacious rumours about lovers' quarrels and even witchcraft.

But to Clare's siblings, it was clear from the outset that her murder was politically motivated. They also believed that the local police force, which continued to be beset by a number of rogue conservative elements during and immediately after the transition, was probably complicit.

As political violence between the ANC and the IFP had gradually consumed KwaZulu and Natal through the early 1990s, there were numerous eyewitness accounts of the security police abetting the IFP. The TRC would later find that 'a network of security and ex-security operatives, acting frequently in conjunction with right-wing elements and/or sectors of the IFP, were involved in gross violations of human rights, including random and targeted killings'.

The frequency of such killings had escalated after the appointment of General Jac Buchner as Commissioner of Police in the homeland in 1990. A former security police chief and ruthless interrogator, Buchner was regarded as one of the apartheid police's leading experts on the ANC. The liberation party described him as an 'efficient killing machine'. It was widely rumoured that Buchner had strong links with the IFP and that officers under his command provided arms to the party. But despite pleas from Nelson Mandela, de Klerk did nothing to intervene in such matters, claiming that many special units had acquired a high degree of autonomy and were carrying out operations on their own initiative.

In Clare's case, there was particular suspicion around a rogue police captain called Rassie Erasmus, who worked alongside van der Westhuizen at the Newcastle Murder and Robbery unit and oversaw Clare's docket. Erasmus was conspicuously unavailable whenever Clare's family went to the police station in Empangeni to follow up on proceedings. The family later learnt from an article in the *Natal Witness* that Erasmus was among the officers who had assaulted Sipho in 1992, leading to his hospitalisation. Erasmus was facing litigation for that assault when he worked on Clare's case. After gathering the initial evidence on the abduction, Erasmus and his colleagues attempted to match Sipho's fingerprints to those on Clare's hijacked vehicle. Her family perceived this as an attempt by Erasmus to use Clare's death to discredit Sipho and effectively clear his own name. It certainly wasn't a stretch to reach such a cynical conclusion. Erasmus had also been censured in court in 1992 for covering up the misdeeds of fellow officers at his precinct.

For his part, van der Westhuizen, a lowly warrant officer, was significantly junior in rank to Erasmus. He was an ordinary policeman, and this put him in a weak and possibly even dangerous position in terms of investigating any allegations that the notoriously murderous local security services could have been involved in Clare's death – its officers were effectively his superiors, after all. At best, van der Westhuizen's investigation was prohibitively slow and insufficiently thorough. A number of key witnesses were never even identified. At the 1995 inquest, six of the witnesses who *had* initially been identified did not appear.

Furthermore, it took the police the best part of seven months to get the petrol attendant, who had lost his job a few days after Clare's disappearance and gone back to his native Swaziland to care for his ailing mother, to return to South Africa to assist in compiling an identikit of Julius. Even once this was done, it would take a further three months for the identikit to be made public, in part because the person responsible for drawing it up went on a few weeks' leave. Van der Westhuizen, meanwhile, was increasingly occupied by another murder case, in Ladysmith, and the various police training courses that formed part of the political transition. All police officers nationwide were also on standby for weeks either side of the elections.

The identikit eventually went out, with a R250 000 reward and an accompanying notice in Zulu, in September 1994. Its heading, in bold capital letters, movingly translated into English as 'Death of a Human Being'.

'On 10 November 1993, Clare Stewart was lost in your place, Manguzi. Her body was found on 24 November. YOU CAN HELP,' the reward notice read.

A single tip-off was received through the associated crime-watch telephone line, which suggested that Clare's murder might have been linked to the unsolved double homicide of two female British tourists on the beach at Sodwana Bay in 1992. This theory failed to gain any traction.

Otherwise, neither the identikit nor the substantial reward yielded any significant new leads. There was a subsequent suggestion that the police had only set such a high reward because they themselves were responsible for Clare's death, so they knew the cash would remain unclaimed.

Even van der Westhuizen went on to note in the summary of his report that it was striking that Clare was generally well liked and had no local enemies. This only seemed to support her family's hypothesis that her death was a political hit. Increasingly frustrated by the police's scant efforts, Clare's aunt Anne contacted Amnesty International, who came to a similar conclusion and launched a major campaign around Clare's case. The organisation's decision was partly based on the findings of a judicial commission of inquiry that confirmed the existence of a 'hit squad' operating within the KwaZulu police, which had been linked to a number of killings in the northern region since 1991.

'Amnesty International is concerned that Clare Stewart may have been the victim of an extrajudicial execution, committed by officially sanctioned covert forces,' the organisation wrote in its first communique about the case in late 1993.

In addition to bombarding Erasmus and van der Westhuizen with mail, the organisation's members also sent hundreds of letters and almost nine hundred postcards from across the world to FW de Klerk and the Commissioner of Police, General Johan van der Merwe. 'You should remember that your country is a member of the United Nations since November 1945,' read one such letter, from a Mr Lezyle Gordon in Invergordon, Scotland.

'I respectfully urge you, on humanitarian grounds, to take all possible steps necessary to arrest those responsible for Clare Stewart's abduction and murder, and to bring them to justice,' wrote Keiko Ito from Tokyo, Japan.

Neither de Klerk nor van der Merwe ever issued any form of response. The latter would resign from his post in January 1995.

In late September of that year, Rosy Parsons, the Amnesty International investigator assigned to Clare's case, conceded that it 'remained to be seen' whether 'in the long run any light will be shed [on the matter],' but she urged members to keep sending their letters.

'I spoke to Rachel today and she sounded quite despondent. She said that Clare's birthday was coming up on Monday 2 October, and she would have been 36 this year,' she went on. 'Rachel was glad that you are continuing your work and grateful for all you have done.'

But at the same time, for all the red flags, Clare's family were loath to push for the murder of a white woman to be prioritised at a time when so many black South Africans were desperately seeking justice for their own lost loved ones. They continued to hope that in due course the new dispensation would demonstrate their professed non-racialism by recognising Clare as a martyr who had served and died for the liberation struggle, and that they would eventually take up her cause accordingly.

But as the months passed with no new developments, the family feared that Clare's death, like so many others in the region, was falling through the cracks of the seismic processes through which democratic South Africa was being wrought.

Part of the issue was undoubtedly the sheer number of cases. But the initial pursuit of justice for the crimes of apartheid after the transition was hampered from the get-go by the departing government's industrial-scale destruction of at least forty-four tons of its state security archive, an act later referred to as the 'paper Auschwitz'.

Furthermore, as South Africa became intoxicated with the utopian promise of the 'new dawn' in the aftermath of Mandela's election, so much of the violence that had beset KwaZulu and Natal was gradually subsumed into a necessarily reductive narrative of reconciliation.

At the eleventh hour, the IFP agreed to participate in the 1994 elections, staving off immediate fears of a full-scale civil war. The party went on to win a narrow majority in KwaZulu-Natal, and thus control of the new provincial government.

Although the bloodletting in the province would never entirely subside, it was gradually pushed ever further from the front pages of the local press. Soon, both the country and the world at large were distracted by the powerful symbolism of South Africa's victorious 1995 Rugby World Cup campaign.

The following year, the Bafana Bafana soccer team won the Africa Cup of Nations, while the IFP and the ANC finally signed a tentative peace accord and began a nationwide disarmament programme.

The hopeful and seductive notion of a new and unified 'rainbow nation', a term coined by Archbishop Desmond Tutu soon after the advent of democracy, was in full swing. But for this to become anything more than a pipe dream, so much of the country's painful past needed to be excavated.

After the frantic first few weeks that followed Clare's disappearance, Themba and Puleng went to live with Rachel in Johannesburg, as Rachel honoured the pact she had made to her sister a year prior to her death.

Having only recently moved back to South Africa with her thirteen-year-old son, Benjamin, and being long since divorced from his father, Rachel was still reeling from Clare's death and was battling to find work. Amid these trying circumstances, she struggled to cope with being a single mother to two additional and much younger children.

'There's such a lot of jealousy and anger floating around the house. Benjamin's jealous of Themba's incursion into his space. He shouts at Themba, who shouts at Puleng, who howls with rage when she is thwarted (a stage, I think), and I shout at them all,' Rachel wrote in a letter to Creina Alcock in early 1995.

A few months later, Rachel and her siblings decided that Themba should be sent to live in Zimbabwe with John and Kathy, whose two children were closer in age to Themba, while Puleng would remain in Johannesburg with Rachel. Two years after Clare's death, it was an excruciating decision for all involved, and the fallout would take many years to heal.

CHAPTER 6

Truth and reconciliation

On the morning of 29 May 1997, Rachel and Peter Stewart walked into a modest town hall in the centre of Mooi River, a small farming town deep in the KwaZulu-Natal hinterland.

It was the final day of what had been a harrowing three-day TRC hearing. The primary focus of the proceedings was political violence between the ANC and the IFP in the nearby township of Bruntville, which culminated in thirty deaths over the course of a few weeks in late 1990. Eighteen of the victims were killed in two days, in what came to be known as the Bruntville Massacre.

More than a year after the TRC began its bold and ambitious quest to help South Africa put its past to rest without going down the route of expensive and politically divisive trials, the Mooi River hearings marked a significant step for the commission. As journalist Max du Preez put it in his introduction to the fiftieth edition of the SABC's weekly Truth Commission Special Report: 'If you were to ask us what the most serious shortcomings were of the Truth Commission we would have to say the lack of coverage of the conflict in KwaZulu-Natal, but this is about to be corrected … The Truth Commission is slowly shifting its emphasis to the only part of our country where the conflict has not ended.'

Du Preez was not overstating the situation in the province at the time. Even as the Mooi River hearings were taking place, a new wave of deadly political violence raged between ANC followers and a nascent opposition party called the United Democratic

Movement (UDM) in the town of Richmond, just over an hour's drive away.

But back in the town hall that day, the mood was subdued. The previous two days' hearings had been hampered by the IFP's refusal to participate in the process, despite TRC attempts to persuade them otherwise. The IFP, however, maintained that the commission was biased towards the ANC and that it would not take part in a process that merely sought to 'reopen old wounds'. This stance was prompted by allegations that IFP leader Mangosuthu Buthelezi had known about police hit-squad activities in the province.

Now, the commission's attention finally turned to Clare. Peter and Rachel both looked anxious as they spoke about their sister's abduction and murder. Having long since given up hope in the police investigation, they were all too well aware that these hearings probably represented their final hope of finding answers to the mystery that surrounded their sister's death.

As Rachel told the commission about the day Clare's body was found, she grew visibly shaken. Her speech was slow and laboured and she grasped nervously at the back of her neck with her right hand. She sometimes trailed off entirely midway through a sentence. Peter would stutteringly pick up where she had left off, his intelligent eyes constantly darting around the room.

The two siblings also provided a detailed written submission to the commission. 'We, Clare's family, want to know who killed Clare, and who planned this murder, especially for the sake of her two young children,' it read in part. 'We would also like work on this case to help clear the fog of political fear that still hangs over this province.'

Their submission went on to list a number of questions about Clare's case that they hoped the TRC might be able to help them answer:

- Was Clare killed on the morning of 10 November 1993? There were rumours that her body had been moved.
- Had the security police known where Clare's body would be found before 24 November?
- How were her hands tied by a single person?
- How did the hijacker stop her jumping out of the car?
- Why did they pick up a hitchhiker?
- Who were the other people seen in the cab of the vehicle on the road down to Empangeni?
- Did the people who enquired after Clare the night before the hijacking have any bearing on the case?
- Did Clare come across sensitive information while travelling around Maputaland?

In mid December 1997, just over four years after Clare's death, the TRC reopened her case for special investigation. Gail Wannenburg and Erik Kjaergaard were the two seasoned investigators assigned to the case. A native of KwaZulu-Natal, Wannenburg had previously done fieldwork for Lawyers for Human Rights in the province and had also worked as an independent violence monitor and election observer in the run up to the 1994 elections. Kjaergaard was an affable and conscientious Danish police detective who'd come to South Africa as part of a delegation of European Union TRC observers.

The two investigators set off for northern KwaZulu-Natal armed with a list of potential witnesses and possible suspects. While in the area, they also planned to meet with Gert Schoon, a former regional commander in the state security services, hoping that he would show them where he and some of his colleagues had blown up the bodies of two other activists, Jameson Mngomezulu and MK Scorpion, in Sodwana Bay.

In a small and overwhelmingly black rural town such as Manguzi, the two investigators expected there would be plenty of murmurings among the locals about what had happened to Clare. But any such hopes were soon tempered by frequent stonewalling and a pervasive climate of fear.

'A major difficulty in relation to this case is that it is alleged that serving policemen in the area are implicated in the murder and witnesses are consequently terrified to come forward,' Wannenburg wrote in her investigation report, which was submitted to the commission on 8 March 1998. 'It is also alleged that policemen have warned witnesses not to speak to investigators, at the cost of their lives,' she added.

Other witnesses gave what seemed to be deliberately contrasting statements, which led Wannenburg and Kjaergaard to wonder if there was some kind of loosely co-ordinated cover-up.

When the two investigators approached officers Erasmus and van der Westhuizen for support with their investigation, they came to share the Stewart family's sense that the two officers were being deliberately uncooperative. Even more suspiciously, they discovered that the AK-47 found in the back of Clare's bakkie was missing from the police evidence locker, as was the associated paperwork.

This was a familiar occurrence in political killings that potentially implicated the security police. A similar situation had occurred with the shotgun used by Civil Co-operation Bureau operative Ferdi Barnard to kill Clare's friend and anti-apartheid activist David Webster in Johannesburg in 1989.

Wannenburg also obtained statements from a few witnesses who claimed they had not been interviewed by the police. Similarly, she found that some of those implicated in the murder had never been traced by anyone working on the case. But despite the numerous stumbling blocks that the two TRC investigators faced, a raft of possible motives for the killing soon emerged, some more credible than others.

Wannenburg quickly dismissed claims that Clare's murder was the result of a lovers' quarrel with Sipho's wife as entirely unsubstantiated. She also found that there was nothing to support rumours that it was an internal ANC killing. The investigators found that both these potential motives seemed to have been propagated by the local police in an attempt to deflect attention from more credible theories.

The most likely of the potential motives, backed by a number of witnesses, remained that the killing was a joint hit by members of the notorious Jozini branch of the security police and local IFP members, either to snuff out any threat posed by Clare's ANC allegiance or to bury sensitive information that she may have obtained while working in the area.

Among other statements from unnamed witnesses in Wannenburg's investigation report, one man who resided near the place where Clare's body was found allegedly saw two police vehicles and a third vehicle, which was presumed to be Clare's bakkie, enter the bushes off the road to Ingwavuma. This witness said he saw a group of white and black men, some of them in police uniform, carrying out what looked like an interrogation.

Although it did not feature in her final report, Clare's family were also informed by Wannenburg that the public road to and from Ingwavuma had been closed for several hours around the possible time of the shooting. Wannenburg inferred that the security police had ordered the closure.

Another anonymous witness statement from a former Special Branch officer stated unequivocally that the security services had been monitoring Clare and had stated that she should be eliminated.

Paul Ngubane, a local ANC member, told the investigators that there had been at least one prior abduction attempt. Another witness alleged that he had been approached by the police to kill Clare, only to become a target himself after disputing the proposed fee for the hit.

Yet another unnamed source claimed that a local IFP councillor called Alfred Mpontshane had tried to hire a hitman to kill Clare. Additionally, Wannenburg's investigation alleged that a 'top official' from Ulundi had come to Manguzi and threatened to send a hit squad to get rid of Clare if the local IFP branch couldn't take care of it themselves.

Wannenburg also acquired Clare's rape docket from the Manguzi police station. Having initially concluded that it had no relevance to the murder and that there were no leads to the alleged perpetrators, Wannenburg changed her mind when she discovered that they were connected to a certain Grace Tembe. Tembe was said to have been involved in surveillance of Clare prior to her abduction. It also appeared that the perpetrators might have been paid to commit the rape. Wannenburg's report also claimed that shortly after Clare's death, various local IFP leaders and businessmen had held a feast to celebrate the recent demise of certain ANC-linked targets, including Clare.

Wannenburg and Kjaergaard also investigated the persistent rumours that members of the cattle project had had a hand in Clare's abduction and murder. The local induna in Manguzi claimed that Khotiza Ngubane, the project's chairperson, had long sought sole administrative responsibility, and that he had mysteriously disappeared for almost a month after Clare's disappearance, only to return flush with cash. The implication was that he had been paid off for assisting with the hit. There were similar mutterings about Jabulani Tembe, who, according to certain strands of local hearsay, had been in a romantic relationship with Clare that had soured.

Despite these rumours, the bulk of suspicion concerning Clare's murder continued to point at the local security police. 'The whole thing [had] a similar modus operandi to other activist killings by the Special Branch in that area,' Wannenburg wrote in her report. Among these was the killing of Mike Mcetywa, the ANC chairperson in Pongola, who was shot and killed in front of a furniture store by a local IFP member on 22 November 1993, just two days before Clare's body was found. A co-conspirator who was in custody for a related murder claimed that Mcetywa's killing was a joint plan by the local IFP leadership and the security police.

Less than two months previously, and a little further south, four executive members of the ANC's Deepdale branch had been shot dead in their vehicle on their way to a political meeting. The ANC claimed this was an IFP hit carried out with the 'absolute knowledge' of certain local police officers.

Wannenburg's report also reaffirmed Clare's family's sense that the police investigation had been at best inadequate and at worst intentionally obstructive.

Busisiwe Mngomezulu, Clare's domestic worker, told Wannenburg that although the police had taken her statement after the abduction, they had never returned to question her after Clare's body was found. Wannenburg discovered that another witness, a teacher called Nandipha Ngubane, who claimed to have encountered a group of men asking where to find Clare's house the night before the abduction, had skipped town. A number of locals claimed that she had fled in response to police harassment.

Wannenburg also collected two anonymous witness statements, both of which indicated the likelihood of a political motive for Clare's murder, from people who had never been interviewed by the police. Dominee van Schalkwyk, another local teacher, told the TRC investigators that it was common knowledge that the Security Branch had had informers within the cattle project and that Clare had been taken out for assisting ANC members in Ingwavuma to hide weapons.

Wannenburg's final report proffered as many as twenty-two possible perpetrators and accomplices in Clare's case. But the most consistently cited in witness statements was a Jozini Special Branch police officer called Aubrey Mngadi, who had worked for Eugene de Kock's notorious Vlakplaas 'death squad' and was well known for his 'shenanigans', as locals put it. Among other statements collected by the TRC investigators, a tavern owner in Jozini claimed he had seen Mngadi drive past in a police con-voy with Clare's bakkie shortly after her abduction. But when Wannenburg and Kjaergaard approached Mngadi for a statement, he refused to meet with them.

Given the overwhelming number of cases with which the TRC was tasked (the commission received more than twenty-one thousand written statements), investigators were often reliant on perpetrators voluntarily offering information.

However, Wannenburg felt that in Clare's case it was not sur-prising that this had not happened. Hers was not an overtly polit-ical killing, and it was uncertain whether the perpetrators would have been granted amnesty through the TRC process. Clare's fam-ily maintained that the perpetrators didn't come forward simply because they felt confident that they would get away with it.

Stymied by the combination of stonewalling and the TRC's time constraints, Wannenburg conceded in her final report that she and Kjaergaard were unable to 'fully investigate' certain leads in Clare's case and recommended that 'the case should be re-opened for investigation with a view to a criminal prosecution'.

By this stage, Wannenburg felt personally invested in Clare's case, in part because her best friend was dating Clare's brother Peter. It also marked a rare defeat for Wannenburg, whose record of solving cases was otherwise near impeccable. So it was that her failure to solve the murder would haunt her for many years, even when a brain disease began to slowly carve large holes in her memory.

Wannenburg also felt great disdain for the numerous per-petrators of apartheid crimes, including Clare's murder, who did not apply for amnesty through the TRC. She continued to hope that one day there would be real consequences for all those who had not respected the process.

Mngadi would continue to stick out for Wannenburg as the one who got away, the key link to the various other pieces of the puzzle that was Clare's murder. As long as he was out there, Wannen-burg believed there was an outside chance that there might be some justice for or, at the very least, some answers concerning Clare's killing.

CHAPTER 7

The farm

About 20 km outside Pretoria, amid the rolling hills of the Skurwe-berg, Vlakplaas perched on the banks of the Hennops River on the outskirts of the small farming town of Eurasmia. At first glance, there was little to distinguish the forty-hectare property from other farms in the area. It consisted of an old, whitewashed farmhouse with a red corrugated tin roof whose awning shaded a long front stoep facing a well-manicured garden.

There were various outbuildings, including a small rondavel. A couple of large Jojo tanks for harvesting rainwater stood sentinel at the back of the property on tall metal platforms. There was also a small vegetable garden and some livestock, which grazed peacefully near the river's edge.

But Vlakplaas was no ordinary farm. It had become state property in 1979, with the express purpose of serving as a base for a new domestic counterinsurgency campaign that sought to deploy 'turned' ANC and Pan-Africanist Congress (PAC) members against their former comrades. These people became known as 'askaris'.

Vlakplaas was the brainchild of a battle-hardened Security Branch general, JJ Viktor, who had learnt during counterinsurgency deployments in neighbouring South West Africa (Namibia) and Rhodesia (Zimbabwe) that captured soldiers could be turned. As he told the TRC in his rather clumsy English: 'I found that many of the people, whether it's ANC, PAC, it doesn't matter … you will find that once … he's returned to South Africa he's very glad to be back here and once you talk to him you will find that a lot of them there are not interested in the struggle anymore. And my idea was why must a man go to jail for maybe 10, 15 years just because he went out for military training ... So, as a detective, as a policeman surely I can use him much better.

'He's been out in the camps there, in Angola or wherever in Africa or overseas, he knows who went with him to the camps. I can assure you that even the more unsophisticated people, they could remember 200 to 250 people who were in training with them. He will give you his name, where he came from, what camps he was in. So that was my idea.'

The Vlakplaas project was initially started with sixteen police officers, all of them askaris, under Viktor's command. He was the sole white officer on the farm. In late 1980, another security services commander, Dirk Coetzee, who'd helped cofound the Vlakplaas project, which came to be known as Section C10, took over from Viktor. The following year, a number of white policemen were transferred to the farm from the ongoing counterinsurgencies on the other side of South Africa's borders.

By 1982, as Jacob Dlamini later wrote in his book *Askari*, 'Vlakplaas and its askaris were considered the "special forces" of the security branch'.

But that same year, Coetzee was unceremoniously removed from his post after the botched abduction of an activist in neighbouring Swaziland sparked a diplomatic incident. Coetzee was transferred to the security police's dog unit, a humiliating demotion. Angry and embittered, he began to openly slander his superiors and was soon discharged from the police department altogether.

The thirty-three-year-old Eugene de Kock replaced Coetzee at Vlakplaas. With his quiet demeanour and thick glasses, de Kock looked more like a dour high school teacher or small-town doctor than someone who would come to be widely known as 'Prime Evil' and have a kill count of at least 120 people. Like a number of young Afrikaner men who came of age in the 1970s, de Kock tried to join the army, but because of a stutter, he was disqualified. He then enlisted in the police force but failed to get into the elite Special Task Force due to his poor eyesight.

De Kock finally rose to prominence within apartheid police structures in 1979, when he cofounded the notorious Koevoet counterinsurgency unit, whose main task was to kill freedom fighters from the South West Africa People's Organisation (Swapo). Koevoet became notorious for its high assassination rate on the northern side of South Africa's border.

Under de Kock, who considered Coetzee a coward for not being willing to get his hands dirty, Vlakplaas became a law unto itself, its increasingly barbarous campaign carried out by officers who were frequently drunk. They would braai chops and drink brandy as they burnt, just metres away, the bodies of men and women they'd tortured and killed.

Thirty-eight-year-old Aubrey Mngadi arrived at Vlakplaas sometime in 1985. A Zulu from the small KwaZulu town of Nongoma, Mngadi had enlisted as a police officer in 1971 and, according to rumour, went on to serve with de Kock. Although Mngadi was a quiet and secretive man, it gradually became clear to many of the askaris and the other black police officers at Vlakplaas that he was a trusted confidant of de Kock's. The commander had recruited him, at least in part, to keep a close eye on his black colleagues and report back as necessary. De Kock admitted as much around the braai one night, after drinking too much wine.

But Mngadi also played an active role in a number of deadly operations during his time at Vlakplaas.

In 1985, he drove several askaris through the Swaziland border post to abduct ANC activist Jameson Mngomezulu. In

June 1986, he was part of a hit-squad operation in Chesterville, on the outskirts of Durban, that resulted in the murder of four United Democratic Front (UDF) activists who were believed to be responsible for killing three white police officers. In August of the same year, Mngadi was involved in the abduction from a Swaziland prison of Glory Sedibe, a senior MK commander who was also known as MK September and who, after enduring severe torture, himself became one of Section C10's most prolific askaris. When Sedibe fought his abductors in the back of the unit's vehicle as they smuggled him across the border, Mngadi smashed a Makarov pistol into the MK soldier's face, rendering him unconscious and leaving him with a long, deep gash down the side of his nose. The scar would never fade.

One of Mngadi's fellow operatives on these missions was Almond Nofomela, who developed a reputation as a notorious Vlakplaas killer, yet also contributed to bringing the entire operation down. In 1987, Nofomela received a death sentence for murdering a white farmer during a premeditated robbery on a farm in Brits. Although neither the robbery nor the murder had anything to do with Nofomela's work at Vlakplaas, during his testimony in court, the policeman claimed that he had become 'desensitised to violence' and regarded himself as 'above the law'. He might have hoped that his influential commander would save him from the hangman's noose, but de Kock soon squashed any such illusions. He sent Nofomela a letter in prison that said there was nothing to be done and that he should 'take the pain'.

On the evening of 19 October 1989, a few hours before he was due to go to the gallows, Nofomela signed an affidavit for Lawyers for Human Rights in which he made startling allegations about the existence of apartheid death squads and his own role in 'approximately eight other assassinations during [his] stint in the assassination squad, and also numerous kidnappings'.

When the *Weekly Mail* published Nofomela's explosive affidavit, his disgraced former commander Dirk Coetzee feared that he would be used as the scapegoat. He fled into exile and confessed everything he knew about Vlakplaas to journalist Jacques Pauw. He had been feeding tantalising titbits of information to Pauw for some years.

On 17 November 1989, Coetzee's story was splashed across four pages of the liberal weekly Afrikaans newspaper *Vrye Weekblad*, which was edited by Max du Preez. The headline read: 'Meet Captain Dirk Johannes Coetzee, commander of a South African Police death squad'. Coetzee famously referred to Vlakplaas as the 'heart of the whore'. He described in gruesome detail the political assassinations, torture, bomb attacks and cross-border abductions carried out by the unit.

By that stage, South Africa's political landscape was changing irrevocably, and Nelson Mandela would be released from prison just three months later.

The Vlakplaas project was shut down in 1993, by which time there were between one and three hundred people classified as askaris on the South African Police payroll.

But de Kock would fight until the bitter end, helping to supply several tons of weapons, including rocket launchers and hand grenades, to IFP leaders, fuelling the escalating political violence in KwaZulu and Natal.

Mngadi, meanwhile, joined the notorious Jozini Special Branch, along with a number of his Vlakplaas colleagues and commanders, in the early 1990s. Here they continued to act as a law unto themselves and carried out a further string of political murders and abductions. After the political transition in 1994, he was integrated into the new South African Police Service (SAPS).

When the TRC hearings began three years later, they gave a fuller account of the atrocities carried out by de Kock and his operatives at Vlakplaas, although only seven of the hundreds of askaris applied for amnesty. At an amnesty hearing at the Durban Christian Centre in September 1999, Nofomela named Mngadi among the operatives involved in the 1986 Chesterville incident. Another of his former commanders at Vlakplaas, Willem Nortje, further claimed that Mngadi had 'gotten very nervous' during the operation and had accidentally pulled the trigger on the 'Uzi machine gun' he was carrying, at which the other members hurriedly opened fire on their targets.

Strangely, Mngadi never gave testimony about his alleged role in the Chesterville incident. However, two months later, he took part in the amnesty hearings in Pretoria where he spoke about his involvement in the 1985 abduction of Jameson Mngomezulu. His sentences were mostly short and monotonous as he responded to the commissioners' questions in Zulu. Although Mngadi admitted to driving the combi that was used to take Mngomezulu across the border, he denied directly participating in the subsequent assault:

> MR NEL: *There has been evidence, especially from Mr Koole, that you took part in the assault on Mr Mngomezulu. Through-out our consultations and what I have put to the other applicants is, you say that you never took part in the assault. Is it not so that if you did take part in the assault on Mr Mngomezulu, you would have asked for amnesty for that?*
>
> MR MNGADI: *I would do that indeed.*
>
> MR NEL: *Were you driven by any spite or malice in taking part in this operation?*
>
> MR MNGADI: *No, I was not spiteful, I had nothing against him.*
>
> MR NEL: *Mr Mngadi, there is one other last aspect. At the time you were a new member at Vlakplaas, am I correct?*

MR MNGADI: Yes, I was still new and I was not quite familiar with the procedures in that place.

MR NEL: And your overall commander was Col. de Kock?

MR MNGADI: That is correct.

MR NEL: Was Col. de Kock at Piet Retief or Jozini or wherever during this operation?

MR MNGADI: He was not there, I did not see him.

MR NEL: Mr Mngadi, are you then asking for amnesty for any offence which might flow from your participation in this operation and also any delict which might stem from your participation in this operation?

MR MNGADI: That is correct, that is why I submitted my amnesty application, because I am involved in this matter, even though I did not lay my hand on Mr Mngomezulu.

The commission would deem that Mngadi, as well as de Kock and Nofomela, among others, had made a 'full and truthful disclosure' and all were granted amnesty. De Kock was also granted amnesty by the TRC for many of his other crimes, although he had already been convicted on 121 separate charges, including six murders and fifty-nine counts of fraud, and had been handed two life sentences plus 212 years' imprisonment in 1996. However, he failed to convince the TRC that any of these crimes were politically motivated, a prerequisite for amnesty. He was granted parole in 2015, after serving twenty years. After his explosive confession, Nofomela's death sentence for the Brits farm murder was commuted to life imprisonment, and he was eventually granted parole in 2009.

Despite their dark pasts and the widespread outrage over their release, particularly in de Kock's case, both men continued to play an important role in providing information on unsolved apartheid-era crimes long after the TRC finished its work.

Mngadi, however, quickly fell out of the public eye after his brief appearance at the hearings, and he left the police force shortly afterwards. But his routine presence behind the wheel during various Vlakplaas abductions chimed with the Jozini tavern owner's statement that he had seen Mngadi drive past in a police convoy with Clare's bakkie on the morning of her disappearance.

Given what emerged in the TRC amnesty hearings, it was unlikely that he had pulled the trigger, but, at the very least, he surely knew who had, and who had ordered it.

CHAPTER 8

Moving on

Cape Town, 2005

Dear Anne,

Clare came into all of our lives through a series of accidents.

The first accident was the visit to KwaNgwanase of an Institute for Natural Resources researcher. He stayed overnight with Vanda and me, and told me over a bottle of wine about how white farmers from outlying areas were starting to visit cattle auctions in Maputaland in search of bargains, because the pure-bred Nguni cattle that were found there were undervalued by their black owners, who during the years of white domination had come to regard anything belonging to blacks as inferior to their 'white' equivalents.

The second accident was that it struck me, that night, that a development project that attempted to capitalise on (and to further improve) the value of the area's bovine bloodstock might stand a chance of social and commercial success, that it might be supported by the members of the black farming co-operative for which I worked, and that it might attract donor funding. All of these 'ifs' turned out to have a basis in reality.

The final accident was that when I mentioned all of this to friends employed by the University of Zululand, one of them – Tessa Cousins – immediately said enthusiastically that she knew JUST the person for the job. And this was Clare, at that time working for a community farming project in the Free State. No. I suppose that that was the second-last accident, really. The final accident was that Clare thought it worthwhile

84

to risk everything by leaving her farm position and coming to a turnkey project in isolated KwaNgwanase.

For it was anything but easy. In the first place, Clare had to go about selling the idea to the farmers who owned Thuthukani, the co-operative. They were not hard to sell on good ideas, but had been burned so often by development projects that were non-starters that they were understandably extremely cautious. So Clare began by taking an elected committee on a road show, around KwaZulu and Swaziland, to see operational Nguni cattle [stud farms] with a view to understanding what it was that constituted success, what pitfalls to avoid, and how to structure such a project's governance.

Despite the fact that a white woman, especially a white woman as unconventional as Clare, was arguably not the ideal person to spearhead such a project, Clare's personality, her commitment and her unswerving integrity won over the people who were to become the owners of the Masivela-KwaTembe Nguni Cattle Project. If ever a white person was loved by the people of KwaNgwanase, it was Clare: and I think that the women found her specially compelling, because while in many ways she did not challenge local notions of femininity – I never saw her wear anything other than a dress, for example – she equally never gave an inch in asserting that women could, and should, take the lead in any endeavour they chose, no matter how much it might once have been thought to be the preserve of men.

If the cattle co-operative survives, it will be because Clare had the vision and the grit to assist its members in shaping it into a sustainable form.

But for those of us who loved her – and there are thousands of us – she will be remembered, too, as an unparalleled friend. I have special reason to be grateful for her unshakeable friendship. It was the early nineties, and the ANC was increasingly making its presence felt in an area where real or pretended IFP affiliation, or at least non-partisanship, had long been necessary strategies for self-preservation. Because of NGO [nongovernmental organisation] turf wars, the project I managed and I had become labelled as IFP-aligned, very seriously affecting our ability to raise funds from traditional sources. On the other hand, my own ANC membership, then becoming increasingly visible, was causing some genuinely IFP-aligned members of the co-operative executive to look seriously askance at me. Both Thuthukani and I were, for a number of reasons, caught between the proverbial rock and the hard place.

Clare, with her MK history, could easily have turned aside from me. But she stayed resolute, because she was a sound political thinker, and understood that the apparent political orientation of impoverished rural people did not make them the enemies of transformation in South Africa; because she knew that our accusers were little more than fair-weather friends to the ANC; but also, I suspect, because it was simply not in her nature to abandon a friend whom she knew to have done no wrong.

Finally, I have a confession to make that I have never before made publicly. It is simply this: while I know that it is egotistical in the extreme to attempt to take upon oneself the unutterably complex happenings of the world, I can't shake off the thought that if I had not thought to pursue the idea of the co-operative, if I had not mentioned to friends that we were seeking a possible project manager, if I had insisted, after the first attack on Clare, that she move into more secure living quarters, she may never have encountered her killers.

I told Clare once of my feelings of guilt, sitting at her grave in the little cemetery at Marianhill, and I don't think that she, with her greatness of heart, holds any grudge against me. But it is not something for which I have yet been able to forgive myself. Perhaps this essay, in this collection of essays, will be the key that allows the healing to begin. I hope so, because Clare deserves to be remembered, not with guilt, but with joy, and with pride.

Warm regards,
Steve Hulbert

On 22 March 2003, Archbishop Desmond Tutu, the chairman of the TRC, delivered its final report to Thabo Mbeki, who had succeeded Nelson Mandela as president in the 1999 elections.

Seven years after the commission was set up amid great fanfare, its closing ceremony was a much more subdued, sombre affair. This mirrored the sense of disillusionment that many South Africans had come to feel towards the process, after years of legal wrangling by a number of the high-level officials it had aimed to expose. It also became clear to the victims that they were unlikely to ever receive any meaningful reparations.

In his press conference after the handover ceremony, Tutu seemed only too aware of the darkening national mood, which was certainly not limited to people's feelings about the commission, but extended to the country's stuttering post-apartheid reality.

'Can you explain how a black person wakes up in a squalid ghetto today, almost ten years after freedom? Then he goes to work in town, which is still largely white, [where people live] in palatial homes. And at the end of the day, he goes back home to squalor?' Tutu asked the crowd of journalists rhetorically. 'I don't know why those people don't just say, "To hell with peace. To hell with Tutu and the Truth Commission."'

But Tutu also took the opportunity to remind South Africans of their victory over the 'ghastly shackles and vicious injustice' of a system whose evil was starkly apparent in the commission's final report, which contained nineteen thousand victim testimonies.

The TRC's final volumes also included the long-awaited report on the inquiry against former president FW de Klerk, saying that he knowingly withheld information from the commission about state-sponsored violations. This had been blacked out from earlier volumes because of a 1998 legal challenge.

The report also reiterated a number of damning charges against the IFP, accusing it of collaborating with white supremacists in the massacre of hundreds of people in the early 1990s. In addition, the commission found that the ANC was responsible for civilian deaths during military operations, killings and maimings resulting from its landmine campaign, and the killing of a number of suspected informers.

Despite this, the ANC continued to increase its majority of the national vote in the third democratic elections, in 2004, which saw Thabo Mbeki re-elected with 69.7 per cent of the vote, up from 66.35 per cent in 1999 and Mandela's 62.65 per cent in 1994.

The National Party, now reformed as the New National Party, had already lost more than half its former support base by the 1999 elections, in large part as a result of de Klerk's retirement from politics in 1997. In the 2004 polls, it took just 1.7 per cent of the vote after forming an alliance with the ANC that angered many of its supporters and led to the party's collapse.

That same year, the IFP lost its majority in KwaZulu-Natal for the first time.

The Stewarts, meanwhile, tried to carry on with their lives. John and Kathy in Zimbabwe formally adopted Themba, and Rachel in Johannesburg adopted Puleng. Given the closeness of the family, the siblings spent school holidays together.

Rachel began a new relationship in 1997 with a fiery Argentinian woman called Lis Lange, who fell in love with Puleng, aged four, at first sight. Rachel and Lis married unofficially in 1999 (same-sex civil unions only became legal in South Africa in 2006). Lis also jointly adopted Puleng when the laws were amended, in 2002.

In the years immediately after Clare's death, her brother Peter had maintained sporadic contact with Sipho, occasionally sending him pictures of Puleng. But Sipho never fully recovered from his traumatic experiences at the hands of the apartheid security forces and continued to spiral into severe alcoholism and depression.

Shortly before the 1994 elections, Sipho had been fired from Cosatu for allegedly using their regional office to hide arms smuggled in from Mozambique, though it was widely believed that he was set up by a colleague at the behest of the security police. For a couple of years, he occupied prominent regional posts in other trade unions, including the South African Commercial, Catering and Allied Workers Union and the Police and Prisons Civil Rights Union. But he remained jaded by his unceremonious dismissal from Cosatu and felt he was overlooked for government posts within the burgeoning ranks of the ANC.

In 1997, Sipho was diagnosed with brain cancer, and his doctor suggested this could have been directly linked to the numerous blows to the head he'd received while in police detention, which had not been adequately attended to at the time. After the diagnosis, Sipho's behaviour and moods grew steadily more erratic until his death a little over a year later, in December 1998. He was buried in the rural village of Nhlalwane near Port Shepstone, where he had spent his childhood before striking out for the city to seek an education and, of course, his fair share of trouble.

By the time the TRC handed over its final report, it was almost ten years since Clare's abduction and murder, yet countless questions concerning the precise details of what had happened to her and why remained unanswered. For her family and friends, as her story faded into the background, this lack of closure irked them, like a piece of gristle stuck in the teeth.

After a number of years, Clare's aunt Anne wrote a biography (never published) of her niece, titled 'To Kill a Laughing Dove'.

She noted in the preface that the intention was to write 'not only about her death, but also about her life, because she was a most unusual and deeply committed woman'.

Anne was an equally unusual and committed woman, and she shared both Clare's affection for cows and her firm belief in the integral role of rural development in building a better world. In fact, Anne and her life partner Sally Timmel cowrote the still-popular series of *Training for Transformation* manuals, first published in Zimbabwe in 1984, which sought to empower oppressed peoples to build creative, self-reliant communities.

Anne had also been a dogged activist in her own right. Following her brother-in-law Jimmy's example, she had joined the National Catholic Federation of Students while studying at Rhodes University, and had then held prominent positions with The Grail, a global ecumenical women's movement, and the Christian Institute of South Africa, a faith-based anti-apartheid organisation. With the latter, in the early 1970s, Anne had personally helped Steve Biko to develop training programmes for the Black Consciousness Movement, which drew on the participatory methods of Paulo Freire. Biko named Anne as one of the two most influential women to shape his life and work.

However, the movement's nine-month training plan was truncated when many of the leaders were arrested by the apartheid police. For her part, Anne was threatened with arrest or banning. She chose exile rather than ceasing her efforts to help black South Africans achieve freedom, only returning to the country in 1991.

Two years later, Anne was the last of Clare's family to see her alive, having flown up from Cape Town to stay with her niece for a few days at Thandizwe at the beginning of October 1993, a month before Clare's disappearance.

Eleven years later almost to the day, in October 2004, Anne returned to Manguzi as she began to write 'To Kill a Laughing

Dove'. By that stage, she had asked Clare's friends and colleagues for memories of her niece (both the good and the bad) and had amassed a number of letters. As her project progressed, she decided that she needed to 'get back into the context where Clare had lived the last four years of her life'.

Almost everyone who was part of Manguzi's small, close-knit and progressive white community in Clare's day had long since moved on. Cally Todd and Laura Campbell, two of the doctors at Manguzi Hospital whom Clare had befriended, had returned to the UK and Ireland respectively. A third doctor friend, Joe Power, had emigrated with his family to Australia. Steve and Vanda had moved to Cape Town in 1995.

The same was true of many of Clare's former colleagues from the cattle project, a number of whom had moved to Durban in search of better job opportunities. However, Anne managed to meet Jabulani Tembe, who was still in town. After Clare's death, he had started a thriving rural development consulting firm and was now a leading light in this field in the province. He told Anne that Clare had had a considerable influence on his career path.

The Masivela-kwaTembe Nguni Cattle Project, meanwhile, was barely functioning. After Clare's death, the stud herd was increased to about seventy head of cattle, but then most of these were sold off after the calves developed a mineral deficiency, because the executive was unable to afford the necessary supplements or additional grazing land required to solve the issue.

Jabulani and Khotiza Ngubane, the driving force of the project in Clare's absence, had both increasingly been pulled into other projects. Jabulani now focused primarily on growing cashew nuts, while Ngubane ran a general dealer store near his property, in addition to working as a traditional healer.

During his lunch break, Jabulani took Anne to Clare's old homestead at Thandizwe.

'The broken frame of the wooden bed had collapsed on the floor. Clare had told me that she was planning to add a small separate bedroom for Themba. I noticed that the foundation had been dug and the first layer of bricks laid down, probably in the six weeks between the time I left and the time Clare died. No further building had been done after that,' she wrote after her visit.

'The place gave one a dreadful sense of desolation and desertion,' she went on. 'It had been abandoned for a long time. Were people reluctant to live there, even to go there, after what happened to Clare?'

PART TWO
Blood

CHAPTER 9

A family affair

I've often pondered the mysterious alchemy that pulls certain people into our orbit at particular stages of our lives. In Clare's case, it was a rather protracted process, her story drifting around the periphery of my world and consciousness for a number of years before some combination of serendipity and circumstance pushed it to the forefront, where it gradually become a near obsession.

I first heard about Clare from Vanda van Speyk and Steve Hulbert, whom I met when I started dating their eldest daughter, Thola, in 2012. At that stage, I had been in South Africa for a couple of years, but hadn't travelled much beyond my base in Cape Town, so I was fascinated by Steve and Vanda's stories from that faraway time and place in their lives. I grew up in a sleepy village in southwest England, so to me Manguzi sounded like a different world in so many ways, yet oddly familiar in others.

I would later learn that Steve, a rotund and wry-witted man who had briefly been imprisoned in the early 1980s for his own anti-apartheid activism, was among the group of local rural development workers who had persuaded Clare to take on the cattle project in Manguzi. At the time, Vanda, an unfailingly kind and measured woman, was working as a physiotherapist in the trauma ward at Manguzi Hospital. Thola was born in the area.

Initially, Steve and Vanda only mentioned Clare's name and her untimely death in passing. Although it was clear that her story still haunted them, to me it formed part of a vague backdrop of violence in their otherwise entertaining tales of rustic rural life shared with an array of colourful characters, or amusing anecdotes involving wild animals.

I first met Themba around the same time. Thola and I, in the heady and hedonistic early days of our relationship, were out with some of her old school friends at a sweaty dive in Long Street when she bumped into him on the edge of the crowded dancefloor.

Thola and Themba had frequently played together when they were little. Vanda told me that a friend of Clare's had affectionately dubbed the pair 'the wild children of Manguzi'. In the decades since, they had barely seen each other, their paths pushed apart by tragedy and displacement.

Thola introduced Themba and we exchanged a few brief pleasantries and awkward smiles – the din of a frenetic Saturday night didn't allow for much else. But even in the low light and my state of hazy semi-inebriation, I remember thinking that Themba was strikingly handsome, with long dreadlocks framing fine features, and that there was something both kind and sad in his eyes.

It was another six years before I had any further contact with Clare's family. In the meantime, I finished my studies at the University of Cape Town and began my first forays into freelance travel journalism. This came about more through chance than because of any strong inclination towards the genre. I then spent much of the next few years gallivanting around east and southern Africa's safari hotspots, mostly working on guidebooks and churning out vapid listicles, before I figured out what kinds of stories I really wanted to tell, and before I felt drawn to Clare.

RIGHT:
Clare's parents' wedding day. Oxford, UK, 1954.

BELOW:
Clare's parents, Jim and Joan, with John at their home in Roma, Basutoland (now Lesotho), 1957.

ABOVE: Baby Clare with her maternal grandmother, Bobby Hope. Roma, Basutoland, 1960.

ABOVE: Clare *(left)* and her sister Rachel. Whittier Street playground, Cambridge, Massachusetts, US, 1963.

ABOVE: The Stewart children, *(from left)* Rachel, John, Clare and Pete. Roma, Basutoland, 1962.

LEFT: *(From left)* Rachel, Clare, Pete and John. Nairobi, Kenya, 1968.

ABOVE: Clare with local boys. Mdukatshani, KwaZulu, 1979.

ABOVE:
Clare's parents, Jim and Joan. US, 1983.

RIGHT:
(From left) Rachel and her son Ben,
Kathy (Clare's sister-in-law) and her
daughter Judi, and Clare and Themba.
Harare, Zimbabwe, 1985.

ABOVE: Clare and Themba at a social occasion. Manguzi, KwaZulu, 1990.

ABOVE:
Clare at Thandizwe. Manguzi, KwaZulu, 1991.

LEFT:
Clare with Themba and Puleng at a friend's house in Pietermaritzburg. Natal, 1992.

ABOVE: Themba in front of the house at Thandizwe. Manguzi, KwaZulu, 1991.

ABOVE: Clare with Puleng. Manguzi, KwaZulu, 1992.

LEFT:
Clare with Themba *(left)*
and Puleng *(right)* at
Thandizwe. Manguzi,
KwaZulu, 1992.

BELOW:
Clare at a community
meeting near Manguzi.
KwaZulu, 1989 – 1993.
*Photograph by Francois
du Toit.*

ABOVE: Clare at work with local men. Manguzi, KwaZulu, 1989 – 1993.
Photograph by Francois du Toit.

ABOVE:
Clare and some of
the co-op committee
members at a community
meeting in Manguzi,
KwaZulu, 1989 – 1993.

LEFT:
Clare's co-op bakkie.
Manguzi, KwaZulu,
1989 – 1993. *Photograph by
Francois du Toit.*

ABOVE: Themba and Puleng *(left)* at Clare's grave.
Marianhill, KwaZulu-Natal, 1994.

ABOVE:
Sithembiso Cele *(left)*, Puleng Lange
Stewart *(middle)*, and Thembalethu Cele
(right). Durban, KwaZulu-Natal, 2021.

LEFT:
Themba at Mdukatshani.
KwaZulu-Natal, 2021.

By mid 2016, I was craving a new challenge. I took on a variety of more ambitious and harder-hitting journalistic projects. Among other things, I embedded with a violent vigilante group in Kimberley, delved into the dangerous world of illegal gold mining in Gauteng, and investigated the alleged murder of a farmworker by a white farmer in the Cape Winelands.

I gradually discovered that I was most interested in stories and places that were largely neglected or misrepresented by the media, but which in some way poignantly illustrated the tension between South Africa's dark past and its increasingly fissured present.

With this in mind, I began to closely follow the dramatic spike in political assassinations in KwaZulu-Natal that characterised both the run up to and the aftermath of the heated local elections in 2016. As the killing carried on almost unabated throughout 2017, the more I read, the more it seemed that so many of the deaths were inextricably linked to the province's history of violence. Yet so little of the media coverage, both local and international, dealt with these links or extrapolated the wider fallout in any significant depth. I saw an opportunity to fill in some of the gaps. I also began to see Clare's story in a new light, her violent demise having occurred right at the nexus between the pre- and post-apartheid eras in the province.

Then, in July 2017, tragedy struck a little closer to home. Steve, whose health had been deteriorating severely for some time, suffered a series of strokes one evening and was rushed to Groote Schuur Hospital, where he slipped into a coma and died in the early hours of the following morning. Though all of us close to him had felt that such a day was increasingly inevitable, somehow it was jarringly sudden when it happened.

I was already thinking and asking more about Clare by that stage, and Steve's funeral brought me into direct contact with other people who had known them both during their Manguzi days. At the same time, Vanda's efforts to track down other lost contacts from the area in order to inform them of Steve's death also appeared to throw up more memories of that period from the recesses of her own mind, some of which she shared with me.

At some point in the months after the funeral, she asked if I would ever consider investigating what had happened to Clare. I sensed she had been building up to asking me for a while, as was generally her way. By that stage, I didn't need much convincing.

With hindsight, I think I was also looking for some kind of distraction. Steve's death seemed to have driven a wedge between Thola and me. In the months that followed, neither of us was able to close the gap, though we were probably both too afraid to fully admit this until much later. Floundering and afraid, I instead shut it out and allowed myself to be consumed by my work, where I felt at least a little surer of what I was doing.

As I did so, an affinity with Clare grew. I was the same age she had been when she died. We had lived similarly intrepid and transient lives, residing in some of the same countries at one stage or an other. And from the still relatively little that I knew about her, we also shared various character traits and worldviews.

At the same time, several pressing questions surfaced. There were the obvious ones around who exactly was responsible for her murder, and what their motives had been. But I also felt a strong desire to better understand who Clare was, and perhaps above all, what drove her. Why had she stayed in Manguzi even after she was raped, and despite all the warnings and the growing precarity of her position?

This perhaps stemmed in part from my own creeping sense of disillusionment with South Africa. By early 2018, I already felt weighed down by the depressingly quotidian violence and injustice I was so often covering in my work. I couldn't tune it out. But by the same token, I was quickly becoming desensitised and apathetic. I felt that I needed to rediscover a clearer and more positive sense of purpose, and this was something that Clare seemed to have possessed in abundance. What had kept her going at a time when so much around her was on the edge of falling apart?

On a clear, sunny morning in August 2018, I drove the short distance from my flat in Lakeside to the bohemian suburb of Muizenberg, whose pastel-coloured houses and intricate streets abut the picturesque False Bay.

A couple of weeks prior, in the first of a flurry of coincidences, I had been talking to a photojournalist friend about Clare's story when he said he had shared a flat with Puleng's partner in Claremont some years previously. He kindly undertook to put me in touch with her. After a brief WhatsApp correspondence, Puleng and I arranged to meet at her home. It turned out she lived just down the road.

After finishing high school at Sacred Heart College, a prestigious and diverse private Catholic school in Johannesburg, Puleng had spent a year travelling and teaching in East Asia before moving to Cape Town at the age of nineteen, to begin a degree in theatre at the University of Cape Town, where she completed her honours. Continuing the family tradition of activism, she had been heavily involved in the #RhodesMustFall student movement in 2015, both as part of the protests and through a series of performative interventions. Although still only twenty-seven years old, she had since established a burgeoning reputation as a boundary-pushing and multidisciplinary artist and filmmaker.

No sooner had Puleng opened her front door than she greeted me as if I were a long-lost friend, wrapping me in a strong bear hug.

Like Themba, she was instantly striking, with short auburn dread-locks, deep brown eyes, a broad smile, and an infectious warmth.

She made me a pot of loose-leaf herbal tea in her bright kitchen, then took me to her bedroom to show me a framed black-and-white picture of Clare that sat atop a chest of drawers. I realised that this was my first real sense of what Clare had looked like. She was somehow exactly as I'd imagined her.

I later learnt that that picture had been taken in Msinga, at the Alcocks' Mdukatshani project, when Clare was about twenty. She wore a loose white dress and sat on her haunches next to a young black boy and a woman who was perhaps his mother. Clare's head was cocked slightly to the side and her face was open and half smiling. She appeared to be listening intently to the other woman, as did the boy. It was a beautiful picture.

It was one of only a few keepsakes Puleng had of her mother. 'Through much of my childhood, she existed mostly as an absence,' she told me, still looking at the picture. As she raised Puleng, Rachel had remained profoundly affected by Clare's death, and she struggled to speak about her sister openly. 'I mostly had to make do with whatever curated bits of information I could get from her other siblings,' Puleng said.

She filled in some of the gaps herself. 'I liked the idea of an MK fighter. I think that was how I mythologised my mother in my teenage years,' she recalled. 'But there was also resentment attached to that. Clare seemed to me then to have made a choice between martyrdom and her children. I found very little solace in that choice, as I was the unchosen. Of course, I realise now that it was not that simple.'

As we moved into a capacious lounge filled with books to continue our conversation, Puleng told me that she had felt a strong pull to better understand her mother – to 'demythologise' her, as she put it – when she had her own children. Ayanda, her eldest, was now three, while her second child, Kaello, had been born just a few months before our meeting and was staring at us wide-eyed from a large, soft cushion next to Puleng on the sofa.

'There was a point where I looked at Ayanda and was very conscious of the fact that he was the same age that I was when Clare died. It broke my heart because he needed me so much. I was the absolute centre of his emotional and physical world,' Puleng said. 'I wanted to make sure that I gave him a deep connection to his past that I felt I had lacked.'

But Puleng was also determined to achieve some kind of belated justice for what happened. 'I always thought that at some point I was going to be able to sit in front of someone and have an acknowledgement,' she told me. 'I do still think that's going to be part of what I do. The more I know about it all, I realise it's a part of what I *need* to do in my life.'

I hoped I would be able to help to some degree on both fronts. But I was also wary of giving any sense of false hope to anyone in Clare's family after so many years, or of dragging up a past that was undoubtedly still profoundly painful. It was a feeling I frequently experienced covering all kinds of stories in the country. I so often found myself asking people – particularly black South Africans – to revisit moments of severe pain and trauma, while simultaneously trying to temper any expectation that doing so might lead to any tangible change or justice.

In other instances, I ended up in the equally awkward position of gently trying to convince people who were understandably jaded by decades of empty words and promises that there was still some value to sharing their stories. Sometimes, I even struggled to believe my own reasoning.

With Clare's story, my sense of discomfort was heightened by my personal proximity to her family through Thola's parents. But I also felt an additional and novel unease stemming from the awareness that the balance of power between journalist and subject was much less unequal in this instance than is so often the case in the South African context. Clare's siblings, whom I knew would be the ultimate gatekeepers of her story, were all highly educated, middle class and white. This had almost never been the case in any of my past work. But I realised that this could also prompt some important and honest self-interrogation, if I was brave enough to go there.

After I had rambled through a long and verbose explanation of some of the above, Puleng told me that she would be happy for me to write about Clare, and about her. She also said she would gladly put in a good word for me with some of her other family members, starting with Themba. It turned out that he lived even closer to me, in a house on the hill about 200 m behind my flat in Lakeside.

Puleng and I made small talk for a while until a bouncing Ayanda returned from school with his father, Jannous. As I left, Puleng said, 'You know, the older I get, the more I think I am like my mother, and I really like that. It's so funny because this is a woman that I obviously don't actually know. But that's also part of the demythologising process that has to happen, I suppose – to see if we really are alike, and how much of who I am really comes from her, and how much comes from myth.'

CHAPTER 10

Red aloes

I sent Themba a message of introduction the next day. True to her word, Puleng had already spoken with him. 'I'm fine to speak,' he messaged back.

We arranged to meet for lunch at a quiet and eccentric bar called A Touch of Madness in the artsy suburb of Observatory, where Themba worked as a production and venue manager for the small, youth-oriented Magnet Theatre.

As was often the case, I underestimated the perpetually terrible traffic on the M3 heading into town from Muizenberg and arrived about fifteen minutes late. Feeling slightly flustered, I walked through the old Victorian building and out onto the leafy terrace at the back to find Themba sitting cross-legged at one of the tables, smoking a cigarette in the winter sunlight.

As he stood to shake my hand, there seemed to be an intrinsic, calm self-assurance about his movements and his general demeanour. But he also immediately struck me as more withheld than Puleng, as someone who is innately aware of how much of themselves they reveal to others – particularly, I imagined, strangers like me, who were eager to dig into their past.

I had a notepad and voice recorder and placed them beside me on the table, but what followed over the next hour felt more as though Themba were interviewing me than the other way around. He asked me a series of keenly considered questions about why and what I wanted to write about his mother. I fumbled my way through the conversation in an embarrassingly waffling fashion while anxiously puffing on a cigarette I'd scrounged from him in an attempt to build rapport.

I could understand his guardedness. To a greater extent than Puleng, Clare's story, and her trauma, were also his own. He had travelled around South Africa with her; he knew the feeling of being sent away to boarding school and pining for her; he had witnessed her rape; he had been old enough to register the rupture that followed her death. It was undeniably easier for Puleng to have a certain detached curiosity about their mother than it was for Themba.

As an intelligent and socially conscious storyteller himself, Themba had reasonable concerns about whether I was the right person to tell this particular story, in all its nuance and complexity. 'No offense,' he said, fixing me with his deep brown eyes, 'but you are a *white man* and you don't speak Zulu. There are going to be things that you will not be able to fully understand or articulate about the world which Clare inhabited.'

I didn't disagree with him. I often grappled with such concerns, as a foreign, English-speaking journalist, in a country where language was so heavily laden with a history of racism and division, and where so much could be lost in translation. Often, when I was interviewing a black Zulu, Xhosa, Sotho or Tswana speaker, I found myself wondering how my identity influenced what they were telling me and the manner in which they told it. What kind of story did they think I wanted to hear? What kind of picture did they want to paint? How much control did they feel they had over their own narrative? And in what ways would this differ if I spoke the same language, or had the same colour skin, or came from the same community?

I had come to accept that any single version of anyone's story was always and inevitably going to be lacking in some way, whoever was extracting it from them. Nevertheless, I told Themba that I believed I could still at least fill in some of the gaps in Clare's story, and that I also felt it would add nuance to the country's narrative.

Themba gradually warmed to me as we spoke, and by the time we said goodbye he had agreed to act as an initial conduit between me and Clare's siblings, who, he said, would be the gatekeepers of her story, at least from a familial perspective.

A few weeks later, Themba forwarded me a short email thread between himself, Rachel, John and Peter. I felt simultaneously flattered and condescended to, on seeing that Themba, more than a year my junior, had referred to me as a '*young* investigative journalist'. But the general response from Clare's siblings was encouraging. 'This looks positive,' wrote John in the perfunctory epistolary style that I would come to learn was shared by all Clare's older siblings.

It was another three months before Themba and I met up again. Just a few days after our first meeting, he went away on a three-week tour with a Magnet production to Japan, and I struggled to tie him down when he returned to Cape Town. Not wanting to pester him too much, I'd turned my own attention to a few other projects that took me back on the road for a while, first in Gauteng and then in North West. Afterwards, I took a few weeks off, and Thola and I got married on a rustic riverside farm in the picturesque Breede Valley.

Themba and I finally met in early January 2019, as Cape Town was emerging from the festive season. On a baking summer afternoon, I walked up the steep hill from my flat to meet him in his Lakeside home, where we sat in the shade on the balcony, drank

Rooibos tea, and smoked a few of the cigarettes that I'd bought to repay him.

After a brief catch-up, Themba brought out a tattered Southern Comfort box full of documents pertaining to Clare's abduction and murder, including copies of the police and TRC reports and the hundreds of Amnesty International letters from all over the world. The box also contained Anne Hope's unpublished 'To Kill a Laughing Dove'. On the front cover of the ring-bound manuscript was a picture of Clare with a young Themba on her lap, his arms raised above his head and looped around the back of his smiling mother's neck.

Themba told me that Anne had entrusted the box to him shortly before her death in December 2015; he was now passing it on to me. 'I knew nothing of its existence before Anne gave it to me. It came out of nowhere and it kind of threw me off balance,' he said. 'My mother's death is obviously something I've known about my whole life, but I never actually had that much information about it, so I initially became a little obsessed. But then I got to a point of saturation, where I wasn't sure I wanted to know more. You know, there are some memories you want to keep and there are some memories you want to let lie.'

By his own admission, up until that point, Themba had spent much of his life trying to distance himself from the memory of his mother. 'I built particular walls and coping mechanisms. I was just defending my emotional self,' he said.

He had also been preoccupied with trying to adapt to a procession of new environments, as he moved from Manguzi to Johannesburg with Rachel, then to Zimbabwe with John and Kathy.

'The thing about moving families often is that you have to learn to assimilate. You become adept at just moving on and shutting out stuff, so I gradually stopped thinking about Clare as time went on,' Themba told me.

In Zimbabwe, he was enrolled in a strict Jesuit boys' school, where the regimented conformity stood in stark contrast to the freedom of his years with Clare in Manguzi, and with the similarly progressive and pacifist leanings of her brother John. 'I couldn't handle that kind of school system at all, so I used to rebel a lot,' Themba said matter-of-factly. 'But I think I was also still just kind of silently withdrawing myself.'

At the same time, he inevitably grew apart from Puleng. Completely inseparable when Puleng was little, the two siblings then only saw each other once or twice a year for a couple of weeks during school holidays.

Themba also remained largely estranged from his biological father, Mosted Venge. 'He'd been to visit a couple of times in my childhood, although he and Clare were separated, but I hadn't seen him for some years. Then, in Zimbabwe when I was around twelve, I saw him driving down the road in front of our house one day. I went inside and asked my parents if he lived in the area. They said he actually worked just down the road and asked if I'd like to see him. I went to see him and that was the last time.'

After graduating from high school, Themba moved to South Africa to study at the University of Cape Town, where he initially started a degree in social sciences, before switching to theatre-making. Even back in his native land, Themba was plagued by a sense of perpetual liminality. 'The concept of home has always been elusive to me,' he said. 'In Zimbabwe, I was always from somewhere else. And here too, I was always from somewhere else. I think Clare felt similarly in some ways, but mine is a multiple in-betweenness. It's a racial in-betweenness, it's a cultural in-betweenness, it's an actual physical in-betweenness.

'It's also a language thing. I spoke Zulu when I was a kid. So the loss of my mother is also connected to the loss of that language, which would perhaps have deepened my connection to this country, or even to my name. I mean, the first thing people often ask me is either "Where are you from?" or "Why is your name Themba?" I hate it. It's like, "Well, that's just my name and I don't owe you the story." No one asks you why your name is Christopher.'

Nevertheless, for the most part, Themba seemed content in Cape Town and with his work in the city's vibrant theatre scene. He was also closer to Puleng, after all their years apart. 'We see a lot of each other now,' he said.

'Initially, we wouldn't talk much about Clare, but just in the past couple of years, it's started to come up more and more. A lot of that started with this,' he added, motioning at the box of documents on the table.

As Themba had waded through the box's contents in 2016, an idea for a play had begun to crystalise. It would deal not only with his mother's death, but also with the broader issues of loss and missing memory in post-apartheid South Africa.

'As I started doing more research, I realised that Clare's death was just a drop in the ocean,' Themba said. 'So as much as it is a story of personal trauma, it is also one of societal trauma. I wasn't alone.'

Themba titled the play *Red Aloes*, for the cluster of those plants growing at the place where Clare's body was found. But wary of elevating Clare's story above others, he cast a talented coloured actress called Iman Isaacs as the lead.

Having created the play collaboratively with his actors, Themba enlisted Puleng's assistance with lighting and set design. She also designed a poster for the play.

Red Aloes was released at the Magnet Theatre in August 2017, garnering glowing reviews from the local press. 'Emotionally drenched, beautifully written and staged,' wrote one prominent

Cape Town arts critic. 'This slow burning meditation on a life remembered ... smoulders with a palpable grief,' opined another.

Drawing on memories from his own childhood, Themba's collaborative production melded physical theatre with poetic, image-based language:

> *I remember hands inspecting the fences*
> *I remember the cattle-co-op*
>
> *Herding the cows into a dip*
> *The vast fields the cows were kept on*
> *I remember a small group of enchanted trees*
>
> *There was a group of huts, the thatched roof*
> *I remember bare feet*
> *The smell of freshly baked bread*
> *The strum of a guitar*
> *Climbing the mango trees by the bottom*
> *Hands shuffling cards*
> *The stream swimming into the natural pool*
>
> *And a smile.*
>
> *I remember her face.*

I started voraciously rifling through the contents of the box the moment I got home, spreading sheaths of paper across my desk and the floor of my office as I tried to piece together some of the different threads and timelines from the police and TRC reports.

Over the following few weeks, I also ploughed through Anne's biography, even bringing it with me as Thola and I departed on a two-week honeymoon road trip up the KwaZulu-Natal coast. Along the way, we spent four days at Sodwana Bay, a stone's throw from Manguzi, and a spot that I later learnt Clare had loved to visit. It was a strange and probably ill-advised experience to be reading about the events leading up to Clare's violent demise in the region at a time when Thola and I were supposed to be enjoying the beginning of a new life together. But by that point, I just couldn't switch off. For much of the trip, I wasn't really there at all.

The book itself spanned a two-week period when Anne went to visit Clare in Manguzi a few months before her death, and primarily comprised a number of conversations between the two women about life, love, politics, and cattle. By all accounts, Anne was an exceptionally intelligent and interesting woman, but she was not a naturally gifted writer. Much of her prose was almost unreadably contrived, particularly the extensive sections of dialogue.

I had hoped that reading Anne's book would give me a greater sense of who Clare was as a person – of the sum of her life and of her character, not just the cold and impersonal details of her abduction and death. However, I quickly realised that Anne was putting her own words into Clare's mouth, speaking for her. Perhaps this was Anne's way of making sense of why Clare had made certain decisions – decisions that led to her death. But it turned Clare into a kind of cipher.

Who gets to tell our stories? This is a pertinent question in the world of journalism, as both newsrooms and their audiences diversify and social media amplifies previously marginalised or misrepresented voices.

Like so many who died prematurely in pre-digital-age apartheid South Africa, Clare never really owned her own story. My telling of it would merely be the latest in a series of appropriations. Although Clare's siblings had been uncomfortable with Anne's account, eventually convincing her not to pursue publication, they too, whether consciously or not, inevitably curated what they told Themba and Puleng about their mother.

Themba was only too aware of this. 'She was always painted as this completely selfless person, but no one is completely selfless,' he had said during our previous meeting. 'I want to know what she was like on a bad day.'

This time, the gap between our meetings stretched to some eight months. The next year, 2019, was a crunch election year in South Africa, and the divisive national debate around land expropriation without compensation was also ramping up, both of which prompted a short burst of augmented attention from the fickle international media and brought me plenty of work. By the end of the elections in mid May, I was already feeling rather burnt out.

I now found that Themba was hard to pin down. There were a few occasions when we made plans, only for him to cancel at the last minute. As much as I tried to reassure myself that he was busy and possibly mildly disorganised, I had a creeping sense that he was withdrawing.

For my part, I felt unusually nervous when I finally walked up the hill to his house again in the soft sunlight of a cool spring afternoon in September 2019. Even while I had worked on other projects over the past months, Clare's story had occupied my thoughts. More than a year on from when I had first met Puleng, I felt inescapably invested. Combined with the familial skin that I now had in the game, my aim of turning this story into something bigger and more ambitious than anything I had worked on before meant that the stakes were high for me.

I was also uneasy about the extent to which my presence in Themba's and Puleng's lives could be influencing both the story I intended to write and their lives more broadly. I tried to be cautious of giving either of them any false sense of hope or unrealistic expectations, but I had little control over what responses my presence and my project might provoke in them. Was it ever possible for it to have been otherwise? The idea that journalists should in no way influence the stories they document is considered to be a central tenet of the profession's code of ethics. But I felt that that was not only mostly an unrealistic ideal in a context like South Africa's, but that it could also be used to abdicate oneself from responsibility.

Themba did little to alleviate my mounting unease about this as we went over some of the gaps in our last conversation. 'You know, you asking me all these questions has made me realise that *I* need to ask more questions,' he said. 'Since we met you, I also think my aunts and uncles have begun to let down some of the walls that they'd built up around Clare's story,' he added. 'Rachel in particular used to be very closed about it, but I think it's kind of been forced back into existence. Just the other day, she started showing me old photos of Clare that I hadn't seen since I was a child. It's the same with my father [John]. For the first time, he showed me photos of the site where Clare's body was found. He's begun to talk about reopening the investigation.'

To Themba, finding out what had happened to his mother remained less important than filling in the gaps in his own history. 'I still have many memories of my mother, but they're often partial or fragmented,' he said. 'Sometimes, I also don't know which are really my memories and which are things that I was told by others that I then made my own. I think memory can be very fickle like that.'

As Themba had explored some of these questions more intimately after Anne entrusted him with the box of documents in 2015, his biological father, Mosted Venge, also serendipitously re-entered his orbit. One of John and Kathy's biological children, Themba's younger brother, had sought a pro bono lawyer for a new venture in Harare and had ended up hiring a young woman who turned out to be Venge's daughter.

At the end of 2017, when Themba was back in Zimbabwe for the Christmas holidays, he had gone to her house for a braai with her friends. 'We got on really well,' Themba said. 'It's funny, we have a lot of similar attributes.'

CHAPTER 11

A reckoning

On the morning of 26 June 2017, a small team of human rights lawyers escorted three grey-haired clients into a high-ceilinged, wood-panelled room at the South Gauteng High Court, amid a cacophony of clicking cameras. A landmark event was about to get underway: the first day of a much-anticipated inquest into the death of the young teacher and activist Ahmed Timol some forty-six years ago.

An apartheid-era inquest had found that Timol had committed suicide after five days in police detention in October 1971, by throwing himself from the tenth floor of the infamous John Vorster Square Police Station in downtown Johannesburg. The new inquest would confirm what Timol's family had always believed: that he was murdered.

Timol may have been the first activist to die in detention at John Vorster, which activists came to nickname the 'Blue Hotel', but he wasn't the last. By the time the doctor and trade unionist Neil Aggett died there at the hands of the security police in 1982, he was at least the fifth detainee to do so, and the fifty-first nationally, since the state had implemented its 90-day detention law in 1963.

The regularity of these mysterious deaths in the grim prisons and detention centres, and the increasingly ludicrous excuses that accompanied them, were poignantly rendered in the widely cited 1979 poem 'In Detention' by Chris van Wyk:

He fell from the ninth floor
He hanged himself
He slipped on a piece of soap while washing
He hanged himself
He slipped on a piece of soap while washing
He fell from the ninth floor
He hanged himself while washing
He slipped from the ninth floor
He hung from the ninth floor
He slipped on the ninth floor while washing
He fell from a piece of soap while slipping
He hung from the ninth floor
He washed from the ninth floor while slipping
He hung from a piece of soap while washing.

In 2003, when the TRC handed over its final report to the National Prosecuting Authority (NPA), it recommended that some three hundred political killings and atrocities, including Timol's and Aggett's deaths, be further investigated, with the intention of possible prosecution. But until the beginning of the Timol inquest in June 2017, these cases had been gathering dust. As this highly symbolic case now garnered belated attention, many of the victims' families claimed in media interviews that the NPA had rebuffed their requests for more information or progress updates on the cases over the intervening years.

Damningly, certain former high-ranking NPA officials would go on to blame political interference for such failings. They argued that the ANC had obstructed their work, for fear that prominent party members could face indictment or be exposed as apartheid informants as a consequence of revisiting these cases.

To a large extent, in the first years after the end of apartheid, the ANC had carefully and successfully built a new national narrative that posited its members as irreproachable liberation heroes. For me, it certainly wasn't hard to believe that they were willing to go out of their way to protect that narrative and, in so doing, keep their hold on power. Given the magnitude and insidiousness of apartheid's evil, it also wasn't hard to see how they could justify any obfuscation of inconvenient truths.

But almost a quarter century on from the transition to democracy, these old cases, and the state's failure to deal with them, were suddenly thrust back into the spotlight by the live-streamed Timol inquest. As such, they would also become a 'proxy theatre of engagement', to borrow the words of apartheid historian Garth Stevens, for a society still riven by racial division, racked by spiralling inequality, and increasingly disenchanted with the post-apartheid project. Essentially, they were seen as emblematic of the country's incomplete healing process.

In February 2018, the corrupt and kleptocratic Jacob Zuma reluctantly resigned, to be replaced as ANC leader and South African president by Cyril Ramaphosa. Ramaphosa immediately faced pressure to address the rot that had set in during his predecessor's reign, including the systematic evisceration of the criminal justice system. He also had to redress the government's broader failure to deal with the historical injustices of apartheid.

In December 2018, Ramaphosa appointed a new director of public prosecutions, the highly regarded former International Criminal Court legal adviser Shamila Batohi. In her first appearance before parliament, in early July 2019, Batohi said the state would belatedly prioritise the prosecution of apartheid-era crimes. By that stage, two years on from the watershed moment of the Timol inquest, another of these unresolved cases was gaining momentum.

In September 1983, Nokuthula Simelane, a bright and ambitious twenty-three-year-old activist, was just two weeks off graduating from university in Swaziland when she disappeared. Her family later learnt that she had been lured into a trap by an undercover Special Branch officer, Norman Khoza, who had infiltrated MK. The abducted Simelane was subjected to months of torture by the security police. Her family would never see her again.

During the TRC hearings almost two decades later, eight officers applied for amnesty for the abduction and torture of Simelane. But the TRC committee declined to grant it for three of these officers – Willem Coetzee, Anton Pretorius and Frederick Mong – when they were adjudged not to have provided a full disclosure.

Simelane's father also testified at the TRC hearings, pleading for the perpetrators to tell the whole truth about his daughter. It was to no avail. He died of a heart attack soon afterwards, in 2001.

By then, there was a growing consensus about what had *probably* happened. Based on various witness statements, as well as the testimony of an anonymous police officer that had been published in the *Sowetan* in 1995, it appeared that Simelane had been shot dead and buried somewhere near the farm where she'd been held captive in Rustenburg. However, her remains were never found, despite the tireless efforts of the national Missing Persons Task Team. This team was set up in 2005 with the mandate to help locate and exhume the almost five hundred people identified by the TRC as having gone missing between 1 March 1960 and 10 May 1994.

In 2015, Thembi Nkadimeng, Nokuthula's younger sister and now the Deputy Minister of Cooperative Governance and Traditional Affairs, filed an application against the state and the NPA, compelling them to act on the case. Affidavits filed in support of this application by Vusi Pikoli, former National Director of Public Prosecutions, and his deputy, Anton Ackermann, brought to light the alleged political interference by prominent figures within the administration of then-president Thabo Mbeki. Among other things, Pikoli's affidavit set out an exchange with former Minister of Justice and Constitutional Development Brigitte Mabandla: 'It would appear that there is a general expectation on the part of the Department of Justice and Constitutional Development, SAPS and the NIA [National Intelligence Agency] that there will be no prosecutions and that I must play along,' Pikoli wrote. 'My conscience and the oath of office that I took does not allow that.'

This commendable stance had negative consequences for Pikoli, resulting first in his suspension and then in his dismissal. But it was too late: the secret was out. The damage had been done.

As I delved further into my research on Clare, I became interested in the simultaneous developments around some of these other more prominent apartheid-era crimes. In mid 2019, I was commissioned to write a story about the issue for *The Washington Post*. I made plans to travel to Mpumalanga to meet Simelane's mother, Ernestine, before driving back to Pretoria to meet one of Timol's nephews, Imtiaz Cajee.

A couple of days before my flight, I paid Puleng another visit. She and her family had moved house and were now in a sprawling property in Rondebosch. She greeted me with a characteristically warm embrace and made us coffee in the kitchen, before giving me a quick tour of her new home. In its various outbuildings, she and Jannous had begun to create a kind of artists' co-operative, or what Puleng called 'an interdisciplinary lab space for people to play'. The space was complete with a music recording studio, another studio for painting, and a spring-floored performance space with a wall-length mirror. Puleng had also been furiously planting medicinal herbs and other indigenous plants in the backyard. 'I'm basically becoming a witch,' she said.

She and I took a seat at a workbench in the paint-splattered painting studio. I could hear Jannous jamming on a guitar while someone else improvised sultry jazz vocals in the next room. The playful tune provided a somewhat incongruous soundtrack to our conversation, which quickly turned to Puleng's determination to seek some kind of justice for Clare. This was buoyed by the growing impetus around cases like Timol's and Simelane's, which Puleng had been following keenly. Beyond the obvious personal interest, Puleng believed that if Clare's case were ever similarly revisited, it could serve a broader social function at a time when the role of women within the struggle, as well as that of white activists, was being reinterrogated by the younger generation.

'We're at a moment where it's imperative to undermine the hegemonic narrative that we've often been given, or to complicate the way that people view what our history was and who it was made up of,' she said. 'It's important to keep injecting people into our history that shake up the idea that it was simple. Because it wasn't. It isn't.'

With regard to most of the TRC cases, the opportunity for any such reckoning was getting precariously small. A number of the perpetrators of these crimes were dead. Of those still alive, many were in their seventies or eighties and were often in poor health. The same applied to the ever-dwindling list of the victims' immediate family members.

In the Simelane case, for example, one of the original accused had died shortly after the docket was put on the court roll in 2016. Simelane's older brother had died of colon cancer the year before that, fourteen years after her father.

Similarly, Timol's father had died a deeply broken man in 1981. His mother, Hawa, followed in 1997, less than a year after she testified at the TRC. The two main suspects in the case, Security

Branch officers Johannes Gloy and Johannes van Niekerk, had died shortly before the reopened inquest in 2017.

Would Clare's siblings also take their unanswered questions about what had happened to her with them to the grave? As things stood, I had no idea if any of the alleged perpetrators of Clare's murder were still alive, let alone where they were or if I could locate them. And what if I did? Would they ever admit the truth? Would anything ever come of it? I began to wonder if I had bitten off more than I could chew. It all felt a little overwhelming.

Puleng, however, was resolute. 'Clare's siblings tried at the hardest and most hurtful time to pursue this thing,' she said. 'Now, it's up to us, her children. It is our responsibility to take up the mantle.'

I was sure Puleng wasn't alone in her thinking. The Timol inquest had undoubtedly galvanised many younger South Africans who had not directly experienced the atrocities of apartheid.

Seasoned journalist and editor Ferial Haffajee, who was working as editor-at-large at the now-defunct South African *Huffington Post* at the time, once recounted how many of the young people in her newsroom were moved to tears by the horrific details of Timol's torture. By contrast, for journalists such as Haffajee, it was all too familiar.

I sometimes wondered about the details of Clare's final hours after she'd left her homestead on that fateful morning. As she sat in the co-operative's bakkie next to her abductors, did she know she was going to die? Was she afraid? Did she try to talk them out of it? Did she try to get away? Was she beaten or tortured before she took the two rounds to the back of her head? It was possible that we would never know.

It was a bright and crisp highveld winter's morning as I flew into OR Tambo International Airport in Johannesburg. I picked up a rental car and hit the road for Bethal, the Mpumalanga farming town where Simelane had grown up and where her mother Ernestine still lived.

In all my years working as a journalist in South Africa, Mpumalanga was the only province I'd never visited. To those in the know, it had some of the most beautiful and geographically diverse landscapes in the country. But like all the provinces, it also had a darker side. It was second only to KwaZulu-Natal in terms of post-apartheid political assassinations, a number of which had been linked to David Mabuza, the current deputy president. It was also the literal black heart of the coal-mining industry and home to twelve coal-powered state power plants. I passed a number of these hulking behemoths as I drove north along a series of arrow-straight roads, regarding them through the car window with unease as great plumes of acrid smoke spewed into the atmosphere.

I also drove through a handful of small and impoverished coal-mining towns that provided a similarly distressing backdrop and were populated by rake-thin and soot-covered men in threadbare overalls.

Bethal and its surrounds didn't appear to be much more appealing. As I pulled into town shortly before midday, the whole place looked abandoned, the streets pockmarked with potholes.

Ernestine lived in a brick bungalow at the end of a quiet street on the dusty periphery of the local township of Emzinoni. She answered the front door with a tired smile, and then disappeared into the bedroom to put in her hearing aids, leaving me to survey her meticulously tidy lounge. One of the walls was covered with a series of large, framed portraits of her four children, including one of Simelane taken not long before her disappearance. Wearing a light-pink dress and close-cropped hair, the young activist looked straight into the camera, with one hand resting on her slim waist and a subtle pout playing across her lips.

Ernestine returned to the room and sat down heavily with a sigh on a green leather couch in front of the wall of pictures. She then recounted the torment that had followed her daughter's disappearance. 'I was distraught. For months, I couldn't stop crying. I couldn't eat. I couldn't sleep,' she said. 'It was during this time that I also began to lose my hearing.'

In 1985, Ernestine suffered a nervous breakdown. She quit her primary school teaching job the following year. 'I didn't have the energy to carry on,' she said.

Fearful of going to the police, given Simelane's known MK affiliation, Ernestine and her husband had instead chased any vague leads they could garner from their daughter's contacts within the ANC. Some of these people had spent brief periods in hiding in the Simelane home, when things had got too hot in the big cities. Over the next few years, these leads would take Simelane's parents to Soweto, Swaziland and Botswana, all to no avail.

'Everywhere I went, people that I met from the ANC kept promising me they would look for Nokuthula and get back to me,' Ernestine said. 'But no one ever did.'

Ernestine had hoped that when the ANC came to power, it would signal a change in her fortunes, but this optimism had proved to be misplaced. She'd remained in limbo ever since.

'I don't want money. I don't care about prosecutions or arrests,' she said, shaking her head. 'I just want to know the truth: where is Nokuthula?' She would repeat this final question at regular intervals throughout the rest of our conversation, the pitch of her voice growing louder and more distressed with each utterance, until, near the end, she was almost shouting it.

After thirty-six years, Ernestine's pain was still so profoundly visceral that I felt like I'd been punched in the stomach. I had to consciously fight back tears. Part of me questioned whether I should have come at all. How many times had Ernestine felt obliged to trot out her trauma for the benefit of strangers like me? How many times had so many bereaved black South Africans experienced something similar? And yet, so often, it had changed so little.

After all the years of fighting with such scant reward, I wondered how much longer Ernestine would keep going. 'When my husband died, I thought I wouldn't be far behind him, but it seems that for whatever reason it was not my time,' she told me. 'Now, I am old and I could die at any moment. I've been punished for thirty-six years. I wouldn't wish such pain on anyone.'

Today, Ernestine's husband and her eldest son are among the various Simelanes spanning a number of generations who are buried in an unkempt and overcrowded cemetery about a ten-minute drive from her home, on the other side of Emzinoni. The week before my visit, Ernestine had made the short trip across the township for yet another relative's burial.

'Before I die, all I want is to know where Nokuthula is buried, so that I can get her remains and bury them there, with the rest of the family,' she said. 'That is a final dignity that we both deserve.'

I arrived back in Pretoria in the early afternoon to meet Imtiaz Cajee at his large suburban residence, where we sat on the stoep while his wife lay on the couch watching TV inside. Imtiaz, who has a round face and short, greying hair, was wearing a bright red T-shirt with 'Ahmed Timol: The Truth Prevails' written across the front in bold letters.

To a large extent, Imtiaz had made his deceased uncle his life's work. In addition to leading much of the legal campaigning in the long run-up to the recent inquest, he had published a book about his uncle's death in 2005, and he had another one on the subject due to be published soon.

'I was only about five years old when my uncle died, but I have faint and very special memories of spending time with him,' Imtiaz told me. 'Afterwards, I used to visit his grave with my grandfather until the age of around twelve. But my family were often very reluctant to talk about what happened. So I started doing my own research as a teenager, collecting clippings and so on.'

After Imtiaz had a nervous breakdown in the early 2000s, he'd decided to apply himself more fully to researching this painful chapter of his family's history. 'I was still grappling with a lot of things that had happened in the country, and was also looking for something productive to do,' he said.

By 2002, Imtiaz had managed to ascertain that some of the alleged perpetrators in his uncle's case were still alive. One of these men, a police officer named Joao Rodrigues, had been interviewed by TRC investigators in 1996. They recommended that he be subpoenaed, but this never happened. Imtiaz wrote to the NPA to advise them that the matter should be pursued. 'They told me they'd failed to establish any new leads and essentially shot the matter down,' he told me.

In 2012, Imtiaz contacted Yasmin Sooka, a former TRC commissioner who'd become the executive director of the Foundation for Human Rights, which sought to provide legal representation to the families of victims of unresolved apartheid crimes. By October 2016, Imtiaz and Sooka's team had compiled enough evidence and applied enough sustained pressure to finally convince the NPA to reopen the inquest into Timol's death.

'By that stage, I'd assumed all the perpetrators were dead,' said Imtiaz. 'But then, I got an email from Rodrigues' daughter, a woman called Tilana Stander, saying that he was still alive. She wrote that her father was a very manipulative man and should be held accountable for what he had done.' (Stander would also open a case of sexual abuse against her father.)

In June 2018, based on the findings of the 2017 inquest, Rodrigues was charged as an accessory to Timol's murder. However, the criminal proceedings were hamstrung by a number of appeals and other stalling tactics used by Rodrigues' legal team.

'I've embraced the fact that we will probably never see him go through a full criminal case,' Imtiaz said. 'But I believe that at least we have given other victims' families hope that they can succeed in finally getting some kind of closure. Without that, I don't think we can ever truly move forward as a country.'

Yasmin Sooka expressed a similar sentiment when I spoke with her a few days later. It would become a kind of mantra to me as I investigated Clare's story. 'For our own shared narrative about the past, these cases are absolutely critical,' she said. 'You cannot build a new society without having a foundation of truth.'

CHAPTER 12

Ballots and bloodshed

Less than three weeks into the Timol inquest, in the late afternoon of 13 July 2017, thirty-five-year-old Sindiso Magaqa parked his black Mercedes M-Class at a spaza shop on the outskirts of Ibisi, a small village of brick bungalows clustered amid the rolling emerald hills of the KwaZulu-Natal midlands. Magaqa and two colleagues, all councillors in the local Umzimkhulu Municipality, were on their way home from a political meeting in the nearby town of Kokstad. The week was almost over and the mood was light. The three councillors, close friends, had stopped to buy snacks and cool drinks before heading to another friend's birthday party nearby.

As they cracked jokes and laughed together in the car, two men in balaclavas stepped out of a red BMW with tinted windows on the other side of the road, brandishing AK-47s. Magaqa clocked the situation before the others – he knew there were people who wanted him dead.

'Be quiet. Don't move. Don't get out of the car. Things are bad. We are about to be shot,' he hissed to his passengers before the gunfire started. More than two dozen bullets ripped through Magaqa's vehicle, most of them aimed at the driver's door, where he was seated. Onlookers scattered or dropped to the ground.

Sitting in the back of the car, Jabulile Msiya closed her eyes, prayed, and waited for it to be over. She was sure they would all die. As the seconds became minutes and the shooting continued, she wondered if she was already dead. Then suddenly everything was quiet. Msiya opened her eyes. She had sustained a gunshot wound to her right shin and a bullet graze on the side of her left calf. Her other colleague, Nontsikelelo Mafa, had been wounded in the leg and hip, but was conscious. In the driver's seat, Magaqa was unconscious and bleeding heavily from multiple wounds to his lower body. Clearly, he had been the primary target of the attack.

Msiya and her colleague managed to drive their wounded friend the short distance to Umzimkhulu's central hospital. Once Magaqa was stabilised, his family swiftly had him transferred to Durban. They were afraid that while he was in Umzimkhulu, the hitmen might get past the hospital's limited security and finish him off.

Despite these efforts, Magaqa died of heart failure two months later. An initial toxicology report suggested that his demise was linked to complications from his wounds, though there were persistent rumours in Umzimkhulu that he had been poisoned in hospital.

Whichever was true, Magaqa's name was added to a growing list of assassination victims in a place where politics was once again proving to be an increasingly deadly game. Four Umzimkhulu officials had already been killed that year and, by late 2018, that number would rise to eight. As such, the town was to serve as a microcosm of the increasingly fragmented political landscape in KwaZulu-Natal.

In contrast to the apartheid era, at surface level, the contemporary violence was often a result of contestation over scarce resources and limited opportunities for socioeconomic advancement, rather than divergent political views. In Umzimkhulu, for example, unemployment hovered at approximately fifty per cent, and the local municipality was the main source of employment, providing jobs to some twenty-one per cent of the population. A government contract or post could provide a rare conduit to financial security for entire extended families.

But to me, there remained a clear link between the political violence that beset the region in the 1990s, and most likely claimed Clare's life, and these more recent iterations. Throughout 2018 and 2019, while I was getting to know Puleng and Themba, I was simultaneously working on a series of in-depth projects about Magaqa and other recent hits with a similar modus operandi. As I delved deeper into the issue, this link between past and present only became more apparent to me.

Staggeringly, since the 1994 elections, there'd been more than five hundred political assassinations in KwaZulu-Natal. Independent crime researcher David Bruce estimated in 2013 that the province had accounted for more than ninety per cent of the political killings countrywide since the dawn of democracy. The numbers could well have been much higher – political motive can be hard to prove.

In recent years, the violence had become characterised by conflicts and power struggles between ANC factions. All the councillors killed in Umzimkhulu, including Magaqa, were devoted ANC members.

Richard Pithouse, the editor-in-chief of *New Frame*, had written about political violence in KwaZulu-Natal since 2001. He told me that this evolution from inter- to intra-party conflict was strongly linked to certain 'central protagonists' in the apartheid-era violence. These people had gone on to become important post-apartheid actors within the ANC. 'The political formation of these figures was fundamentally shaped by the civil war in the province,' he added.

A former IFP military leader called John Mchunu came to play a prominent role in the violent political evolution of the ANC in KwaZulu-Natal. As the apartheid state crumbled in the early 1990s, he had joined the ANC, along with many other IFP members. He went on to become a leading regional figure and a key mobiliser for the 2009 election of Jacob Zuma.

Pithouse wrote of Mchunu and other former IFP members who were united in support of Zuma that they brought a 'politically authoritarian, socially conservative, and acutely patriarchal' nationalist aspect to the forefront of the ANC. This often resulted in scant tolerance for dissenting voices, not only outside party ranks but within them too. By the time Mchunu died in 2010, he was alleged to have helped establish a powerful system of economic and political patronage in KwaZulu-Natal, which was consolidated through strong links to organised crime. All this provided fertile ground for the ongoing militarisation of politics in the province and inculcated a culture of political assassination.

The ready supply of firearms from the struggle days only exacerbated the issue. The disarmament and demilitarisation process begun in 1995 had failed to account for a large number of these weapons, which were still being used in contract killings. Many of them, in particular AK-47s, had passed through the porous borders of neighbouring Cold War proxies, including Mozambique and Angola. There were rumours in towns across KwaZulu-Natal of these firearms being buried in backyards and of large caches hidden in caves and in the forest undergrowth.

I often wondered what happened to the AK-47 that was presumed to have taken Clare's life, after it disappeared from the police evidence store. Perhaps it, too, had returned to criminal hands and continued to play a role in more recent political killings.

In the first half of 2018, some months before I met Puleng, I made a couple of week-long reporting trips to KwaZulu-Natal to investigate the spate of killings that had occurred in the bloodiest months before and after the 2016 local elections. Magaqa undeniably had the highest profile of any of the victims. He was seen as a rising star in local politics: in addition to being a councillor, he was a former secretary general of the ANC Youth League and a close friend of Julius Malema.

With this in mind, I made Umzimkhulu my first stop. On a sweltering March afternoon, I met Jabulile Msiya at her squat single-story home. It was perched on a steep hillside on the edge of town, overlooking sprawling farmlands and the river from which the town took its name.

Msiya was a former secondary-school teacher and a dogged grassroots campaigner for better public schools and services. She'd been inaugurated as a councillor for her third straight term after the 2016 elections, winning eighty-two per cent of the votes in the small ward in which she lived. The median age of the nine thousand residents was twenty-two.

Msiya, a diminutive and soft-spoken woman, had an air of quiet self-assurance about her. Her long dreadlocks were tied back in a tight bun to reveal a striking face and prominent cheekbones. Before we settled down to talk, she pointed out an imposing concrete building down the hill from her house. 'This is the house Magaqa was building for his family. We were going to be neighbours,' she said. Instead, with the construction work now abandoned, the grey shell served as a reminder both of Magaqa's premature death and the constant threat that local political figures faced.

As we spoke, two of the four children that Msiya had raised as a single mother, as well as the bodyguard appointed to protect her since Magaqa's death, watched television together in the lounge.

Msiya believed that her friend was killed for his strong stance against corruption in an area where graft was both commonplace and highly lucrative. 'He would fight against anything that was not right, that was against the principles of the municipality,' she said. Msiya claimed that the person who had ordered the hit on Magaqa still worked side-by-side with her in the municipality, but she was afraid to name this individual or provide further details, for fear of reprisal. There had been no arrests in connection with any of the political murders that occurred in Umzimkhulu in 2017.

Meanwhile, there were still vacant political offices within the municipality. Two opposing factions had emerged, with diverging views as to who should fill these posts, mirroring the wider divisions within the ANC between supporters of Zuma and Ramaphosa.

With new officials due to be sworn in soon, Msiya worried that more violence was on the horizon. But despite the risk, she said her family continued to support her political career. 'They are always praying for me. They say, "It's God who put you in this position, so don't allow your enemies to make you leave this job. Just continue. We will support you. We will be behind you."'

The picturesque farming town of Richmond was my next destination. About two hours' drive to the northeast of Umzimkhulu, it sits in a verdant valley surrounded by undulating fields of sugar-cane and plantations of towering eucalyptus and pine trees.

As I drove out towards the hillside township of Ndaleni, with early-morning mist still hanging over the area, groups of men and women waited beside Richmond's main thoroughfare to be ferried to work in overcrowded flatbed trucks.

A solitary bulb cast a sterile light over the front door of Thandazile Phoswa's former home, a whitewashed bungalow with panoramic views of Richmond and the surrounding hills. The view was spoiled by the jagged razor wire wrapped around the property's perimeter. The house, now empty, served as a macabre monument to Richmond's long history of political violence, and its intergenerational impact.

In 1997, Phoswa's mother and father, as well as two of her younger siblings, were slain in front of her in their home during an outbreak of violence between the ANC and the recently formed UDM. Phoswa was seventeen years old at the time. She had already lost an uncle and an aunt in an outbreak of fighting between the IFP and the ANC in 1991. That violence had claimed more than 100 lives in Richmond in less than six months. Another 120 people would die between 1997 and 1999.

Then, late one night in April 2017, thirty-seven-year-old Phoswa – a staunch ANC loyalist and Richmond's deputy mayor – was shot in the head in the same living room where she had watched her parents die. She became the second of three ANC political figures to be killed in Richmond in less than three months. This had followed two similar murders in late 2016, raising concerns that history was repeating itself in an area once considered the epicentre of KwaZulu-Natal's so-called 'killing fields'.

Andrew Ragavaloo was the town's mayor in the late 1990s, at the height of the violence between the ruling party and the UDM, which had been led by notorious warlord and disgraced former ANC figure Sifiso Nkabinde. Many Richmond locals told me that Ragavaloo must have lived a charmed life to still be alive today. Most of his closest political comrades had not been so lucky, including his brother-in-law and former deputy, Rodney van der Byl, who was shot twenty-seven times, outside his home in May 1997. Nkabinde eventually shared a similar fate, when more than eighty high-velocity rounds tore into his body as he left a local supermarket on 23 January 1999.

I met Ragavaloo in an air-conditioned office at the Richmond Traffic Department, where his son Dwayne was the managing officer. Ragavaloo had a broad nose, a crooked smile, and a booming voice. He was a keen orator and liked to expound on Richmond's complex history in long monologues. He was also the author of a 2008 work of nonfiction, *Richmond: Living in the Shadow of Death*, about the violence in the town. 'Richmond is what I always refer to as a dormant volcano,' he told me. 'Things bubble away beneath the surface for a long time, until suddenly it just explodes.'

Though Ragavaloo – now sixty-seven years old – had retired in 2016, he had continued to keep his finger firmly on the pulse of local politics. He believed that Richmond's violent past still played a role in the more recent politically linked assassinations.

'That history is still with us, because there's a lot of anger and resentment amongst those victims and the families. They never received any sort of counselling or reconciliation. Homes were burnt down and never replaced. Entire families were wiped out. It was complete overkill. During that time, you could buy an AK-47 for about R50 – that's how cheaply life in Richmond was regarded,' he said.

When I left Ragavaloo, I drove up the hill to Ndaleni to meet Thandazile Phoswa's uncle, Ulwazo, as he returned home from work. After shaking my hand and welcoming me into the lounge, he unclipped a holster containing a 9 mm pistol from his belt and handed it to his wife, asking her to put it away in a drawer in the kitchen.

A similar pistol had been used to kill Ulwazo's niece. It was registered to Phoswa's boyfriend, a private bodyguard named Samkelo Chili. Although Chili was placed at the scene of Phoswa's death by a number of witnesses, he had claimed that Phoswa had used his firearm to shoot herself in the head. Chili was charged with contravention of the Firearms Act for failure to lock his gun in a safe. But the murder charges against him were dropped in late April 2017 because of insufficient evidence, prompting violent protests by local ANC supporters outside Richmond Magistrates' Court.

Ulwazo, who had raised Phoswa after her parents' death, rubbished claims that she had shot herself, saying that it would have gone against both her strong Christian values and her political ambitions. He also dismissed rumours that her death was the result of a 'lovers' quarrel', as suggested by some tabloids at the time. I thought of the similar rumour, dismissed by the TRC investigators, regarding Clare's murder. Instead, Ulwazo believed that Chili, whom Phoswa had been dating for three months, had been 'deployed' to carry out a hit on her.

'Some days before she passed away, she told the family that she knew there were some people who wanted to kill her, but she didn't know who or why,' Ulwazo told me. 'We advised her to leave town for a while and go somewhere safe, but she refused.'

I asked Ulwazo and his wife what kind of a person Phoswa had been, and they both laughed. 'What I can say is that she was a very stubborn person – a straight talker. She didn't tolerate any nonsense,' Ulwazo eventually said, with a wry smile that suggested Phoswa could be a handful. 'She was always fighting for the community, fighting for service-delivery. She was a leader. She was a very strong woman.'

Subsequently, a local ANC councillor, who spoke to me on condition of anonymity, said that Phoswa was rumoured to know who was responsible for the murder of Richmond's former municipal manager, S'bu Sithole, and was intending to speak out. Sithole was shot dead about a month before Phoswa.

The councillor also suggested that Ragavaloo was in some way connected to both these murders. He alleged there was an argument between Ragavaloo and Sithole, while Ragavaloo was mayor, over the awarding of a municipal tender to a service provider that Sithole felt had dubious credentials. The councillor claimed that after Sithole's murder, Ragavaloo had become a silent partner in this company.

'Ragavaloo is a very intelligent person, but he's also a very dangerous person. All of these bad stories in Richmond are attached to him in some way. But you never know how he gets away with it,' the councillor told me.

Two more of the 2017 murders also fitted the pattern described by the councillor. Sifiso Mkhize was shot eighteen times on his way home from a community policing meeting, having only recently entered the political fray after previously serving as Ragavaloo's personal bodyguard. Mthulisi Ngcobo, the municipality's former head of security, worked with Dwayne Ragavaloo and was shot dead outside his home in Ndaleni in late 2015. Dwayne had himself faced murder charges after fatally shooting a man in a Richmond tavern in 1999. He had claimed self-defence and was later acquitted. That same year, two of Ragavaloo's former bodyguards were involved in the assassination of his nemesis, Nkabinde.

A number of other Richmond residents I spoke to shared the councillor's sentiment that neither Ragavaloo nor his son were to be trifled with. Most were too afraid to speak about this on the record. One resident believed that Ragavaloo had used his book to distance himself from Richmond's history of violence, paint Nkabinde as the sole villain, and claim the moral high ground. But wider scrutiny of the period revealed that remarkably few political figures had escaped without any blood on their hands. Was Ragavaloo one of them?

Some weeks later, back in Cape Town, I called Ragavaloo to put some of the councillor's allegations to him. He was relatively candid about his personal connections to some of the victims and perpetrators of the violence in Richmond, but flatly refuted claims that he was in any way implicated in murder. 'If it wasn't such a serious situation, in that many people died, I'd treat it as a joke, a bit of twisted humour,' he told me, adding that people were 'grasping at straws to deflect from the real situation'.

Phoswa's boyfriend, meanwhile, remained the only suspect arrested in the latest spate of violence in Richmond, and all the cases were still open. History certainly didn't inspire confidence that these cases would yield results: only twenty-one of the 120 murders in the late 1990s saw convictions, and eleven of those were from a single crime scene. Similarly woeful conviction rates were mirrored across much of KwaZulu-Natal, where the endemic culture of impunity only served to further fuel the violence.

As was the case during apartheid, the suspected widespread collusion between the police and nefarious political players certainly didn't help. Veteran scholar of policing, Bill Nixon, succinctly encapsulated the politicised role of the police in places like KwaZulu-Natal in this way: 'The police are more likely to police for a specific domination in the interests of a dominant class, race, or other social group in unequal, divided societies.'

There were, of course, still conscientious officers out there, but they faced a range of obstacles. A few days after leaving Richmond, I had an illuminating conversation with three police detectives in Durban from a special task force assigned to investigating political killings in KwaZulu-Natal. They spoke to me on condition of anonymity.

We met at the back corner of a large car park outside the city's central police station. The three men seemed deeply fatigued. They told me that their investigations were routinely hampered from the get-go by the unwillingness of witnesses to come forward, even when offered witness protection. 'People are afraid. They know that they could also be eliminated if they give testimony,' one of the officers said.

For their part, the officers were twitchy and voiced fears for their own safety. 'When you are working on political violence, you are always on the lookout. It's a very risky business. Our families are very worried about us,' another of them told me. 'Even you yourself, when you wake up in the morning, you don't know whether you are going to come back home in the evening or not.'

I returned to KwaZulu-Natal a number of times over the next year to cover various aspects of the political violence. This culminated in an in-depth documentary on the subject for *Al Jazeera*, which aired in early 2020 and featured Jabulile Msiya as one of the main characters. With each visit, I found that the fear and paranoia voiced by the three detectives, among many others, had become increasingly contagious. Whenever a car appeared in my rear-view mirror, particularly at night, I prepared myself to take evasive action. When an unknown number flashed up on my cell-phone screen, I half expected it to be an anonymous death threat.

A number of the people I spoke to made it clear that I was being watched. And so I got used to meeting sources in strange places and to venues being changed at the last moment. I also got used to the omnipresence of heavily armed personal security details when I was interviewing politicians or other powerful figures. On a few occasions, they were around regularly enough for me to end up befriending them.

The more time I spent in the province, the more difficult it became to see how it could ever pull itself out of the perennial cycle of violence. The constant stories of death and impunity started to wear me down. A similar despondency also seeped into my work outside the province. I became cynical and jaded, a common but unattractive trope among journalists working in harsh environments.

Again, all this brought me back to thinking about Clare. As I increasingly questioned my own professional motivations, I felt a growing need to know the depth of hers. Did she have similar doubts or moments of despondency?

It was there, in that far-flung place, that she had found the sense of purpose and belonging she had so long sought, even as the province, and the country for that matter, was burning around her. Did she cling to it until the bitter end? Did she feel defiant as her hands were bound and a gun put to the back of her head? Or did she feel resignation, or even regret?

I didn't believe that I knew enough about her to hazard a guess. Perhaps I never would. But I was more determined than ever to try and find out.

CHAPTER 13

Leaving

Less than two kilometres from Puleng's house, the squat grey Clareinch Post Office sits on a busy street corner between the Claremont Police Station and Livingstone High School, and a couple of blocks away from Oblivion, a popular student bar. In the early afternoon of Saturday 24 August 2019, nineteen-year-old University of Cape Town film and media student Uyinene Mrwetyana walked into this typically nondescript government building to collect a package.

A forty-two-year-old post office employee called Luyanda Botha told Mrwetyana that the electricity was out (not an immediately suspicious assertion in the midst of frequent rolling blackouts) and that she should return later and he would assist her then. When Mrwetyana came back a little after 2 pm, Botha was alone in the post office. He invited her inside, locked the door and proceeded to attack and violently rape her. When Mrwetyana wouldn't stop screaming, Botha bludgeoned her to death with a heavy scale. He carried the young woman's body to the trunk of his car and drove to open ground near his home in Khayelitsha. There he burnt her corpse. When he was arrested a week later, police found blood still inside the post office and on one of Botha's shoes.

In a particularly cruel irony, not lost on women's rights activists, Mrwetyana's murder took place in the final days of the annual Women's Month. She was not the only woman to meet such a gruesome end over the course of those four weeks of often super-ficial pageantry and lip service. According to police statistics for the preceding twelve months, a woman had been murdered every three hours.

But there was something particularly disturbing about the way in which Mrwetyana met her end, not in some poorly lit back alley in the depths of night, but in broad daylight in her local government post office, a seemingly benign sanctum of quotidian banality. It highlighted, among other things, the fatal flaws in the often victim-blaming arguments about where women should and shouldn't go, what they should and shouldn't wear, who they should and shouldn't talk to.

Poignantly, at Mrwetyana's funeral, her mother told the mourn-ers that she was sorry that she hadn't been there to protect her daughter, and that, of all the places she had warned her about, the post office wasn't one of them.

This seemed to mark a breaking point for the country's women, who lived with the constant threat of rape and femicide. A wave of protests erupted that garnered global media attention. There had been countless similar protests before, but as I spoke to friends and colleagues in the aftermath of Mrwetyana's death, many of them agreed that something significant had shifted. As Capetonian writer Rosa Lyster put it in a thoughtful piece for *The New Yorker*, it was 'as if the flashover had occurred, the point where the fire in the room becomes the room on fire'.

In Cape Town, thousands of people marched on parliament to demand a more definitive and urgent response to violence against women. They were met with the usual platitudes from President Cyril Ramaphosa, who received a memorandum with a list of demands, including that a state of emergency be declared. As he addressed the enraged crowd, they responded with loud boos.

Puleng and Jannous were among the protesters, as they so often had been ever since their Rhodes Must Fall days. Themba was also there, having cancelled a lunch I'd scheduled with him.

A week later, recently having returned from one of my reporting trips to KwaZulu-Natal, I met with Puleng at her Rondebosch home. It was a perfectly clear Cape Town winter's day. We sat in the sun on a bench in her garden and drank strong coffee. Puleng was in an uncharacteristically sombre mood. She told me she was rattled by what had happened to Mrwetyana, and the fact that it had occurred just a stone's throw from where we sat.

A few days after the news of the murder emerged, Puleng's home was broken into. She awoke in the night, with her children asleep on either side of her, to find two men in balaclavas in the room, one of them armed with a knife. He pointed it at Puleng and held a finger to his lips warning her to keep quiet, then they slunk out of the house with Jannous' laptop and made off in Puleng's car.

Puleng knew only too well that it could have been much worse. 'That's the crazy thing, though,' she told me. 'If you *don't* get raped or killed when something like this happens, people will say you were lucky. That's not normal. It's not normal that because of the country I live in, and because of what happened to my mother, I am constantly holding my breath waiting for my own violent death. But that's the state of being a woman and a woman of colour in South Africa.'

Puleng admitted that after the break-in, for the first time in their eight-year relationship, she and Jannous had had a serious conversation about the possibility of moving their family overseas. But even entertaining such a thought left Puleng feeling an acute sense of guilt and shame. After all, this was a country where the vast majority would never have that option, and where the notion of emigrating was so often associated with embittered, racist white people.

'Rachel tried to reassure me that I was still young and that I didn't owe this country anything, but I'm still made to feel shitty essentially just for wanting to feel safe. At the same time, I acknowledge the immense privilege it takes for me to have even been able to have that conversation with Jannous. So while I am deeply, deeply sad about this place right now, I don't like the person that wanting to leave makes me out to be.'

Even as a non-South African, I found myself grappling with similar feelings. As far back as 2015, I had written a post on my rather angsty and now-defunct blog admitting that 'for the first time since I left England on a one-way ticket and decided to make South Africa my home five years ago, over the past few days more than once I've caught myself wondering, even if only for a second, if it's time to give up and move back. But I haven't told anyone this because I'm ashamed by these thoughts.'

The blog post ended on a hopeful, if somewhat self-referential, note with my decision to stay put for the time being. Unexpectedly, it went viral and was republished by *Daily Maverick*.

It was the first and still the only time in my life when, on more than one occasion, strangers recognised me in bars (thanks to an accompanying profile photograph on the *Daily Maverick* site) and spoke to me about my work. I also received hundreds of emails from South Africans all over the world grappling with their own feelings of guilt and shame around 'abandoning' their country.

There were scores of other mails from recent returnees who had optimistically decided to give South Africa another chance after being away for years. Once I had shared their optimism, but that seed of uncertainty about whether this place was where my future lay had grown until it had become almost all-consuming.

Puleng said she felt she had to 'put one or two good things in place' before she could seriously think about leaving. Her comment reminded me that Clare had been planning to leave

Manguzi as soon as she felt that the cattle project could sustain itself without her. I wondered if, had Clare survived, she would have followed through. So many people had tried to convince her to leave. She held out for achieving her goal, but it was easy to see how any such an end point could have become a constantly shifting horizon. She had spent much of her adult life seeking a place of belonging and purpose, and that place and that project was where she had finally found it. I had also once felt like that about South Africa, but now I spent much of my free time talking and fantasising about where else I could go.

Puleng seemed to read my thoughts. 'Whatever happens, I do not plan on becoming a martyr,' she said emphatically. 'I will not second-generation that, even if that means I have to give every-thing up and take my children somewhere else.'

I also wondered how Puleng's life might have been different if Clare had eventually left Manguzi and moved to Pietermaritz-burg, or anywhere else for that matter. I asked her if she ever thought about this, and she said that sometimes she worried that posing such questions could destabilise the happiness and contentment she had created.

It was clear that she was fiercely protective against anything that might negatively impact upon her children. At the same time, she reiterated that having children was precisely what had sparked her interest in knowing more about Clare and about her history in the first place. In fact, she was considering making a documentary film about Clare. 'I'm trying to demythicise my mother and create a person that I can understand and find connection with,' she said. 'I also want to scrutinise this idea of Clare as a *character* rather than a real person in my life.'

There was, of course, also the whole other side of Puleng's identity that she knew even less about, and this too had resurfaced within the previous few weeks.

In late August, Puleng had received a friend request and a message on Facebook from somebody called Thembalethu Cele. He claimed to be the first-born son of Sipho Cele, Puleng's father. He said he had accompanied Sipho to Clare's funeral as a shy thirteen-year-old, as well as on a couple of trips to Manguzi, where he remembered meeting Puleng as a baby.

Puleng clicked on Thembalethu's Facebook profile and was immediately drawn to the cover photo, a dated black-and-white image of a striking man in a white collared shirt with angular features, an egregious smile, and a short, neat goatee. 'It was the first time I had ever seen a proper picture of my father,' she told me.

She and Thembalethu had a long and emotional WhatsApp conversation, during which he told her that one of the last things Sipho had said to him was that he must find Puleng and make sure that she was okay. 'It was a big deal, because I'd always thought that side of the family was actively not interested in me,' Puleng said. 'But as someone who would like to think that they are a whole, filled-out person, it is also unnerving to dig back into this unknown side of my past and consider how much that might inform who I am.'

Since her conversation with Thembalethu, Puleng said she had tentatively thought about taking a trip to Durban, where Thembalethu was based, to meet him and possibly some of the rest of her father's family. But she was also unsure what she would represent, or what kinds of expectations might be placed on her, as a 'light-skinned artist from Cape Town'.

'There's a whole process that must happen there, a whole other part of myself that I still need to grapple with,' she said, her eyes widening at the expectation. 'But knowing that and doing the work are two different things.'

CHAPTER 14

Sisters

I pulled onto the curb of a narrow, leafy street in Claremont just before 10 am on a Monday morning. Finally, more than a year after first meeting Puleng and Themba, I was meeting Clare's sister Rachel, at the home she shared with her wife, Lis. As had been the case with Themba, I suspected our first meeting would be less an interview and more an opportunity for her to suss me out and pose some searching questions about my intentions and my approach before she assisted me in any way.

I'd had a couple of brief phone conversations with Clare's brothers John and Peter in the preceding months. These days, John was teaching English in Saudi Arabia, while Peter, whom Puleng had once referred to as the 'mad scientist' of the family, lived in Johannesburg and was a professor in the Department of Development Studies at the University of South Africa (Unisa). I found common ground with John talking about our school cricket careers and our respective familial affinity with the UK – his to Cambridge, where he was born, and mine to Devon, where I grew up, and Oxford, where my mother now lived with her second husband. Peter was a little brusquer and cagier, but seemed satisfied that I wouldn't make a complete hash of Clare's story. I would speak to Alice, Clare's younger sister, who still lived in the US, where she taught English literature at a high school, many months later over a video call. Open and talkative, she was still moved to tears when she recalled the trauma of losing her older sister.

As far as Rachel was concerned, both Puleng and Themba had repeatedly warned me that she was the most reticent of the siblings when it came to talking about Clare's death. She was an experienced book editor, and a former journalist to boot, which I imagined might add another layer of scrutiny to our encounter.

I rang the bell beside the front gate and heard dogs barking inside the house. As soon as Rachel opened the door, two large ridgebacks raced out to greet me. 'I hope you like dogs,' she said as she welcomed me inside, her accent still distinctly influenced by the erudite intonations of her upbringing in England and some of its former colonies.

Based on the few pictures I had seen of Clare, I quickly noticed that she and Rachel had the same eye colour: a hazel brown that turned to green in bright light. They also shared the same assertive jawline. In the footage from the TRC hearings in Mooi River in 1997, Rachel had long auburn hair. She now wore it short and gelled into tousled grey waves above her bespectacled brow.

We sat down on either side of a dining table and, as I'd done with Puleng and Themba when I'd first met them, I prattled on for a while about why, what and how I intended to write about Clare. Rachel also probed me about my background and politics, the latter of which I reassured her were progressive and left wing. By the end of our conversation, I could see that she still had reservations, and that it had not been an easy encounter for her. Nevertheless, she was willing to meet with me again for an interview, and she asked for a list of questions and talking points in advance. The door had opened a fraction.

We met at Rachel's house again two months later, in December 2019, as the first cases of the novel coronavirus were being detected in the Chinese city of Wuhan, though that was still way off my radar. As before, I was greeted at the gate by the two ridgebacks, Asterix and Trotsky.

Again, we sat at the dining table. Rachel pulled out some old newspaper clippings about Clare's abduction and murder, as well as an array of photos of Clare at different ages. In the oldest of the bunch, a black and white image taken in Zimbabwe in 1986, Clare and Rachel stood side by side smiling at each other. Rachel looked tall and glamorous in a tight black blouse and white pencil skirt with her long, thick hair hanging down to her shoulders. Clare was a little shorter and wore her hair in a bob with a straight fringe. Her hands were thrust into the pockets of a dress patterned with guinea fowls. A young Themba stood beside Clare, staring straight at the camera while inserting what looked like a toy car into his mouth. 'Clare was less full of herself, less assertive, less confrontational than I was,' Rachel said as she looked at the image, 'but she was also profoundly stubborn.'

The most recent photo in the pile showed a fuller-faced and curlier-haired Clare on the beach at Kosi Bay in August 1992, a month after Puleng was born. Rachel, who was still doing her master's in England, had returned to South Africa after Puleng's birth to spend her summer holidays with Clare at Thandizwe.

Rachel recounted how Clare had proudly showed her the Nguni herds grazing on the project's lands. The sisters had also explored Kosi Bay in Clare's beaten-up VW Beetle and swum in the warm Indian Ocean at Sodwana Bay. Clearly Clare took great pleasure in showing people the things and places she loved. 'We had a wonderful time,' Rachel said. 'I think that in many respects Clare was happy with her life in Manguzi.' It was already apparent to Rachel then, however, that Clare was in a precarious position.

'She was ANC aligned in an area that was becoming increasingly politically volatile,' she told me. In addition, Themba was now at boarding school almost seven hours' drive away – the main reason Clare was thinking about leaving. 'But at the same time, I think she had really found meaning in what she was doing in Manguzi, so it certainly wasn't ever going to be an easy decision,' Rachel said.

It was during that time together that Rachel and Clare made their fateful pact that should anything happen to Clare, Rachel would take care of Themba and Puleng. 'It certainly wasn't a fleeting thing,' Rachel said. 'It was real. We both realised that it might happen.' Taking seriously the things that really mattered to her, after all, had always been part of Clare's makeup. 'Even though obviously not everything in her life was totally planned, there was a certain consistency in Clare's choices and in her political principles that ran all the way through her life, which I think is quite remarkable,' Rachel said. However, she also told me that Clare would have worn the label of 'activist' reluctantly. 'I've always felt that it's a rather elastic word,' she said.

The word was first used in the early 1900s to describe Swedes who advocated that Sweden should abandon neutrality and enter the First World War on the side of the kaiser. In its subsequent usage it became part of the lexicon of the 1960s, as civil rights and anticolonial movements swept the globe. Today, the word is malleable, and often self-appointed: a catch-all term for all manner of political and social movements and forms of collective action. But while this is part of its appeal, it can also be both self-serving and reductive.

'Clare was so much more than just an activist,' Rachel said. 'And at the same time, I don't think she felt that the way she had chosen to live her life was remarkable.' She conceded, however, that Clare never spoke to her about her role in MK, even though it was Rachel's then-boyfriend who had recruited her.

As I considered what Clare might have kept from her family, I asked Rachel about Puleng's teenage resentment towards her mother based on her sense that she had chosen her activism over her children. For the first time in the interview, Rachel bristled with frustration and defensiveness. 'There have been various people over the years who have criticised Clare for having children and then still getting involved in the struggle, but for goodness' sake, imagine if everyone who had a family hadn't got involved,' she said.

I wondered aloud whether these kinds of sentiments were reserved for the women in the struggle. It was hard to imagine the same criticism being levelled at a man. 'Oh yes, I think there's certainly a degree of inherent sexism to it,' Rachel said. 'The thing is that for the most part the children have been fine. I mean, of course, they had a very painful thing happen to them and it has reverberated through their lives, but they are *fine*.'

Although it was certainly true that Puleng and Themba both seemed to be mostly well-adjusted, happy people, I wondered if Rachel was veiling her own lingering pain and trauma, which Puleng maintained was something she had never really dealt with. This stemmed not only from the loss of Clare, of course. Within the span of less than ten years, Rachel had also lost both her parents, walked away from an abusive first marriage, and then gone through the heartbreak of parting with Themba.

She admitted that, like her mother, she had suffered from bouts of depression through much of her adult life. 'I think Clare also struggled with her own sense of depression, and her own sense of not being able to assert herself and so on,' she added. 'But nevertheless, she achieved a lot.'

Rachel reiterated that for the most part, Clare did the bulk of this on her own. She recounted a story of Sipho coming to visit Clare in Mtunzini, some weeks after Puleng's birth, with a pair of baby socks that had the word 'Daddy' written on them. To this, Clare took great umbrage. 'By that stage, she and Sipho had broken up, and to Clare it was very clear that Puleng was going to be *her* responsibility. I think Sipho had provided Clare with a bit of relief in her life after the rape, but it seemed to me that Clare had always fully intended to raise her children alone.'

That trip to Manguzi was the last time Rachel saw her sister alive, but they continued to keep in regular contact via letters and phone calls. 'Work is going well. Real steps forward are being taken – cattle soon!! Puleng is well and happy. For that matter, Themba is also happy – just away. I find that so hard,' Clare wrote in one such letter in January 1993, before ending with her typical sign off: 'Very much love, Rachel, I hope you are happy.'

A few days before Clare's disappearance, Rachel phoned her from Johannesburg, where she was staying with their brother Peter. She had recently returned from the UK. During the conversation, the sisters hatched a number of plans, including a week-long break at Lake St Lucia and then a family Christmas with all of the siblings in Johannesburg. They also discussed the possibility of moving in together in Pietermaritzburg.

But when Peter told Rachel that Clare was missing, on the evening of 10 November, Rachel told me she had immediately feared the worst. 'I felt sure that it was a political killing, and I didn't expect a lot from the police as I knew they were usually behind these kinds of things,' she said. 'There were of course the various other theories about muti or suggestions of a love triangle, but I never believed any of those. The same goes for any suggestion that the ANC played some part in her death.'

I wondered about Rachel's certainty on this last point. As recently exposed by the revisiting of other apartheid-era killings, including Nokuthula Simelane's and Ahmed Timol's, the ANC had some skeletons in its closet. Also, if we were to accept that there had been rogue security police officers in KwaZulu and Natal conducting their own operations without the official sanction of the central government, was it not naïve to assume that the same couldn't apply to the ANC?

Furthermore, the spate of witch killings carried out in Manguzi in the early 1990s, most of which had been attributed to an ANC-aligned youth group, served as but one illustration that political interests and affiliations were rarely entirely detached from other cultural and social factors. Rachel herself alluded to the blurry lines between politics and culture in the region when she told me that there were 'people who didn't like women, people who didn't like white people, people who didn't like the project, all of which provided fertile ground for Clare's death'.

It was easy to see why Clare's family were reluctant to point the finger at a political movement whose cause their sister had so wholeheartedly supported, to the point of being willing to risk her life for it. I also wondered to what extent TRC investigators like Wannenburg, who saw apartheid's violence up close and personal all across KwaZulu-Natal over a number of years, might have brought certain unconscious biases into their investigations.

If Clare was killed, as many people have suggested, because she had seen something she shouldn't have, in a place as lawless and awash with guns as KwaZulu, was it not plausible that this could have been something to do with the ANC? After all, there was significant suspicion around Jabulani Tembe, who, in addition to being Clare's assistant and the cattle project's administrator, was an active ANC member. This suspicion was not definitively dispelled by Wannenburg's investigation. Perhaps it was wrong to think of an alleged power struggle within the project and an internal ANC hit as necessarily distinct motives for Clare's killing.

I continued to ponder Rachel's comment about the various factors that had provided 'fertile ground' for the murder as I drove home from her house. I'd also noticed a certain contradiction in many people's sense of how Clare and the cattle project were perceived in and around Manguzi. On the one hand, I was told that she had been widely accepted by the community and that the project had managed to remain apolitical. Even van der Westhuizen, the police officer who worked on Clare's case, had remarked in his report that Clare was 'well-liked' and had 'no local enemies'.

On the other hand, a broad spectrum of people could be said to have potentially wanted her dead. Wannenburg's TRC report proffered as many as twenty-two possible perpetrators and accomplices spanning the political and social spectrum.

There was also a second contradiction: while people claimed that Manguzi was a generally safe place where Clare had felt at home, at the same time they highlighted the precarity of her position and her own sense of feeling dangerously exposed. Perhaps, as when attempting to draw a line between politics and everything else in a time and place of such significant rupture and flux, I needed to accept that something could be many things at once.

When I got home, I found that Rachel had sent me a scan of a short story about Clare written by her friend Laura Campbell, the visiting Irish doctor who had driven Puleng from Manguzi to Jane Quin's house in Shongweni after Clare's disappearance.

The story had appeared in a collection called *This is how it is: true stories from South Africa* in 2018.

'I want to describe her so you care,' Campbell wrote. 'I want you to see her, to visualise her standing in the sweat of her cotton dress and in the dust of her flat shoes. She deserves so much more than me sitting here scratching around in my memory for hints and traces of her.'

As I read the story, I realised that Clare was nowhere to be found in these pages, as she was nowhere to be found in Anne Hope's book. As with Anne's book, the dialogue attributed to Clare felt contrived, created by the author to feed a romanticised *idea* of Clare. There were also factual errors. Clare's first name was spelt incorrectly as Claire; her nationality was attributed as Zimbabwean; Themba and Puleng were misremembered (or recast?) as Bongani and Pumi; the location and circumstances of Clare's murder were fudged.

It struck me that the Clare of Campbell's imagining, as was the case with Anne's, had never really existed. According to the psychological scientist Robert Neimeyer, grief regularly involves 'processes by which meanings are found, appropriated or assembled' into a memory. Other psychologists argue that grief can also impair one's ability to retrieve autobiographical memories altogether.

I wondered how much of the retrieval of South Africa's history, like Clare's, had been impaired by a collective, societal grieving. And I felt daunted as I considered that perhaps my job in writing about Clare was not to draw from the memories of Clare's family and friends, but to fill in their gaps, and even to challenge their falsehoods.

PART THREE

Homecoming

CHAPTER 15

People don't talk

By all accounts, in the twenty-eight years since Clare's death, the once-sleepy town of Manguzi had changed significantly. Among other things, a raft of new supermarkets and fast-food outlets had sprung up along the now-tarred main thoroughfare. In between the gleaming facades, scores of traders, most of them women, crowded the pavement, sitting next to voluminous piles of cheap clothes and handbags.

Now replete with lodges and guesthouses, the area was a hub for tourists exploring the nearby golden sandy beaches and lush nature reserves, or making a last pitstop before heading across the border into Mozambique. (That country had undergone its own gradual tourism rebirth since the end of its decades-long civil war in 1992.)

But pieces of Manguzi's troubled past remained, albeit sometimes in a slightly different guise. The area was still a hotspot for cross-border crime and trafficking, while the chronically under-resourced and underpaid local police force was routinely beset by corruption. (In 2017, eighteen police officers were arrested for colluding with cross-border car-theft syndicates implicated in a raft of violent hijackings in and around Manguzi.) The local ANC-run municipality, riven by factionalism and ravaged by graft, was frequently the target of service-delivery protests and shutdowns by poor black residents.

I decided to make my first trip to Manguzi after a frustrating few weeks of failing to track down Clare's former colleagues from the cattle co-operative, as well as anyone from the area who might have known anything about her abduction and murder. Many of these people had fallen off the map altogether, which was unsurprising given the decades that had elapsed, let alone the fact that, as a border town, Manguzi was a transient place. Its population had also been devastated by the Aids epidemic of the early 2000s. Even now, HIV prevalence in KwaZulu-Natal was about thirty per cent.

For her part, Vanda had long since lost touch with any of her old contacts from Manguzi. She gave me a list of names, but most were common Zulu monikers that turned up scores of results in my Google searches. There was little I could do about Clare's story from the comfort of my small office in Muizenberg. I needed to visit the place where so much of her legacy both began and ended.

But as I drove through the centre of town, slowing occasionally to allow goats and cows to cross the road, I felt anxious. In my career as a journalist, I had never pitched up somewhere new or unknown with so little to work with. I had no sense of whom I could trust or rely on. And I was a little raw from my recent experiences of reporting on political violence in other parts of the province.

I was also chastened by a Google Maps-related mishap en route to Manguzi that had culminated in my small rental car getting stuck in a patch of deep, soft sand some kilometres from the nearest tarred road and any kind of cell-phone service. A group of burly young Zulu men had eventually come to the rescue, literally lifting the car out of the sand and setting it on a firmer track, but my ego did not emerge unscathed from the debacle.

Thankfully, I was not alone in all this. I'd enlisted the assistance of Zimbili Vilakazi, a soft-spoken and prolific Durban-based freelancer. Zimbili was a minor local celebrity in KwaZulu-Natal, thanks to her work for the popular *Daily Sun* tabloid. There she covered everything from taxi violence to tokoloshes, sometimes filing as many as four stories a day. On our way to Manguzi, we were more than once accosted by a petrol attendant eager to know what story she was working on.

While Zimbili rode shotgun, my nomadic photographer friend Sam sat in the back of the car, regaling us with anecdotes from recent reporting trips to far-flung places, including Nepal and Ethiopia. A little closer to home, Sam and I had recently finished a series of articles in Durban for *GroundUp* about the shack-dwellers' movement, Abahlali baseMjondolo. They were locked in an increasingly bitter land conflict with the ANC and eThekwini Municipality. At least ten Abahlali leaders had been killed since 2013, while the group's irrepressible secretary general, S'bu Zikode, had survived a number of attempts on his life and was currently in hiding. The plight of Abahlali was inextricably linked to other forms of state corruption and political violence playing out across KwaZulu-Natal, with many of the same power brokers and trigger pullers involved. The rot was everywhere.

I had, at least, managed to line up one apparently solid source in Manguzi. He went by the nickname Makotikoti and was widely rumoured to make his living as a wildlife poacher. He was also said to have been an active part of local IFP paramilitary groups in the early 1990s. Another journalist colleague, who had spent some time doing a documentary on turtle conservation in nearby Sodwana Bay, assured me that Makotikoti knew pretty much everyone in the area, including many of the more unsavoury characters.

We met Makotikoti at a busy Engen petrol station and then followed his beaten-up Toyota bakkie to a mud-brick bungalow a couple of kilometres out of town. Chickens wandered around the periphery of the property, pecking at the sandy soil. Makotikoti invited us into a dank and dimly lit living room, where an elderly man with cataracts sat in an olive-green armchair near the only window. As we spoke with Makotikoti, the old man would occasionally interject distant and fragmented memories in Zulu to no one in particular.

Makotikoti, who had small eyes, angular features, and a deep scar running down the right side of his face, had only vague recollections of Clare. However, he did know a former member of the cattle co-operative called Mandla Ntuli. This man now worked as a lawyer in Durban, but he often returned to Manguzi to see family or for business. After I'd taken down Mandla's number, I asked Makotikoti in a fairly roundabout way about his memories of the violence between the ANC and the IFP in the early 1990s. He stared at me impassively as he responded to Zimbili in Zulu. Even though I didn't speak the language, I could tell that he was evading the question. 'He says that he doesn't remember much,' Zimbili eventually translated. 'He says it was a very long time ago.'

I called Mandla the next morning. He was in Manguzi for a couple of days to attend a funeral, which happened to be taking place down the road from our accommodation on the edge of town. He stopped in for a coffee and a chat once the proceedings were over.

A portly and convivial man now in his early fifties, Mandla had worked as a driver and fixer for Clare back when he was still a bookish eighteen-year-old. 'She was a very likable person,' he recalled. 'She tried as much as possible to be part of the community. And she was always trying to improve her Zulu so that she could converse with people freely in their own language.'

Mandla also said that Clare had helped him and other similarly politicised locals to set up one of the first ANC Youth League branches in the area. 'But in terms of her own ANC affiliation, she was not a revolutionary activist, she was more of a quiet activist,' he added. 'Her kind of activism was just to sit with people as if she was one of them, to treat everyone equally.'

Mandla had left the co-operative and moved to Durban to study law before Clare was killed. In fact, she had helped to fund his studies and had connected him with Peter Rutsch, a friend who was an attorney with the Legal Resources Centre and with whom Mandla had done his articles. Mandla did remark that a number of rumours about the motive for the murder had continued to circulate in the area for some years after he left.

One such rumour was that the co-operative's chairperson, Khotiza Ngubane, had had a hand in Clare's murder to consolidate his own power, and that her assistant Jabulani Tembe may also have been involved. 'There were certainly differences within the co-operative from time to time,' Mandla said without mentioning any names. 'To my mind, they likely came about because there were resources that Clare had brought to the table that people wanted to appropriate for their own benefit.'

Mandla maintained that a political hit carried out by state security services in conjunction with local IFP structures was the most likely explanation for Clare's killing. However, it was not implausible that these forces could have identified and potentially exploited any weak links or divisions within the co-operative for their own ends.

Mandla didn't have a number for Khotiza, but he knew where he lived, and gave me detailed directions. If I got lost, he said, I would just have to mention Khotiza's spiritual name, Mbekaphezulu, and anyone in the area would be able to help me find him.

Mandla also gave me the contact details of a local ANC stal-wart called Mcabango Mthiyane, who'd been born and raised in Manguzi and still worked in the local municipality. Mcabango had known Clare personally, and Mandla assured me that he was also a fount of knowledge about some of the shadier things that had gone on in the area back in the 'old days'.

Mandla spoke of his youth in Manguzi with obvious nostalgia. He believed it had always been a peaceful and close-knit place at heart, and that Clare had felt this too. The violence, he main-tained, was 'thrust upon' Manguzi by external forces. 'Things have certainly changed a lot since then,' he went on. 'In those days, you could almost count on your hands the number of people who had any kind of education or formal qualification. Nowadays, there are plenty of university graduates around, not that most of them can find any work of course.'

When Mandla got up to leave, I noticed that the owner of the lodge was eavesdropping on our conversation from behind the bar. As I paid our bill, he took the opportunity to probe me about what I was doing in town – I imagined he didn't encounter too many journalists sniffing around here. The same could probably be said for most small towns in the province, if not right across the country. In so many of these places, some of the most pressing issues were being played out at the local level almost entirely unnoticed by the rest of the country, while most of the media industry chased pontificating politicians from one drab press briefing to another in the handful of major urban hubs.

Perhaps my own rural upbringing was part of what drew me to more peripheral locales, in tandem with a stubborn and prob-ably self-righteous determination to always go against the grain. Whatever you put it down to, I was always happiest working in places where I was unlikely to bump into another journalist.

However, it could sometimes be both a blessing and a curse. While the novelty factor often made people much more open to talking to me, it also made it hard to keep a low profile.

The intrigued lodge owner was himself a recent arrival in the area from further down the coast, near East London. To him, Manguzi was a laid-back and friendly place, and he was surprised to learn of its violent past, which he said was certainly not something he'd ever heard locals talking about. He suggested I contact an ex-police officer called Ian Smith, one of his regulars at the lodge bar, who he said might have more insight.

He gave me Smith's number and I called straight away. Smith was amiable enough, but said he had only moved to Manguzi in the late 1990s, and he claimed not to have heard of Clare. But he told me of another ex-police officer, called Lappies Labuschagne, who had worked for the security services in the area in the early 1990s. Smith didn't have his number but said that he still lived in the town of Jozini, some hundred kilometres away. It wasn't a lot to go on, but I felt I was finally getting just a little closer to the scent.

I pulled up at the Maputaland Lodge, at the end of a potholed road just off Manguzi's incessantly busy main drag, late the following morning. A large and unflattering carving of an elephant with a missing tusk greeted me at the entrance to a gravel car park, where my tiny hatchback looked comically out of place amid a cluster of bakkies. In rural towns, I often found that the car park told me the kind of clientele I could expect to find inside a bar or restaurant. Suffice to say that as a left-leaning journalist from the city, and an *Engelsman* to boot, a car park full of bakkies often filled me with a certain amount of trepidation.

Sure enough, as I walked into the lodge's bar – a tall, thatched building with Springboks and Blue Bulls flags hanging from its wooden beams – I immediately felt the harsh glare of a handful of large and po-faced Afrikaners in two-tone shirts and velskoens who were dotted about the place drinking brandy and Cokes and chain-smoking cigarettes.

I ordered a Coke from the gruff bartender in my very limited Afrikaans and slunk outside to sit at a table near the swimming pool, away from any prying eyes.

I was at the lodge to meet Mcabango Mthiyane, Mandla's ANC contact. It was easy to spot him when he walked in a few minutes later. He was the only black man in the place, but he carried himself with a certain swagger. He good-naturedly laughed off a few jibes from one of the older white men propping up the bar about the municipality's poor service-delivery record and Jacob Zuma, then took a moment to greet the other drinkers, all of whom he knew by name. Then he saw me waving at him from outside and walked over to join me.

Mcabango was a professorial-looking man in his mid sixties with a greying beard, a slightly lazy right eye, and the calm but calculated demeanour of a career politician. From the late 1970s through to the early 1990s, he was a regional MK leader in the area, frequently jumping back and forth across the Mozambican border, often with illicit firearms or other 'materials', as he put it, in tow.

In 1990, Mcabango was charged with a murder in Pongola, which he insisted he had had no part in, and spent much of the subsequent six years in and out of various jails and courtrooms across the region. The charges were eventually dropped, in the aftermath of the 1996 local government elections.

Shortly afterwards, some local police sources told Gail Wannenburg and Erik Kjaergaard, the TRC investigators, that Mcabango was also considered a suspect in Clare's murder. It was alleged that he had approached Clare to help cover his bail costs while he was in prison for murder, but that she had refused, provoking violent retribution. But the two seasoned investigators concluded that the theory was far-fetched and was more likely a red herring cooked up by Special Branch officers to throw them off the scent.

'The security services is certainly where I would point my finger,' Mcabango told me. 'Clare was working closely with us in the ANC and in the underground in those days, and the police were certainly well aware.'

I liked Mcabango immediately and wanted to take him at his word throughout our conversation. But then, every so often, he became vague. I was also aware of how difficult it was to ever know who you could really trust in the province's political sphere, given the corruption, the political killings, and so many unsolved crimes, both past and present.

I read Mcabango my list of other potential suspects in Clare's murder, but he said that most of them had moved on soon after the 1994 elections. 'They took an early pension or retirement package,' he said, 'and then they disappeared.'

But even in their absence, Mcabango said, a culture of fear and silence persisted around the area's history of violence. 'Most people don't ever talk about the past,' he said. 'I don't think the TRC did their work properly. There's still a lot of information hidden under the carpet here, and a lot of people are still afraid.'

The Khulumani Support Group, founded to assist those testifying before the TRC in the late 1990s, estimated that about eleven thousand of the almost twenty-two thousand human-rights-abuse victims that the commission had identified were from KwaZulu-Natal. As Mcabango implied, many of these victims were never included in the subsequent TRC public hearings. Instead, their wounds were left to fester.

Many of the central protagonists of the violence had also slipped through the net. Some were quietly subsumed into the newly legitimised state structures. Others went on to occupy prominent positions in the upper echelons of the provincial government.

'Some of these people have a lot to lose and they don't know which cases might rise up again,' Mcabango told me. 'Maybe they still talk about the things they did in the past,' he added, then a wry smile crept across his face. 'But if they do, it is only when they are alone.'

CHAPTER 16

The sangoma

There is something poignant and deeply jarring about the wild, sand-swept landscapes of the KwaZulu-Natal coastline, about the stark contrast between their rugged beauty and the history of violence for which they have so often provided the backdrop.

As we drove down a winding dirt road flanked by rolling dunes that took on a bluish hue in the soft morning light, we passed several derelict buildings, many of which appeared to have been abandoned decades ago. I found myself wondering what had befallen their occupants – which of the province's various scourges had spirited them away. Political violence. Aids. Poverty. Migrant labour. As they departed to their next destination, whether ethereal or earthly, were they aware of the beauty they were leaving behind? Could they still see it?

While entertaining these whimsical thoughts, I had missed the unmarked turning to Mbekaphezulu's house, and we were now lost. In this respect, journalism could be a frequently humbling profession. Almost daily entering new and unfamiliar environments, I spent so much of my time lost in one way or another, and often the only way to become less lost was to admit my ineptitude to others.

In this instance, there was a part of me that was secretly happy to delay our arrival. After all, there was a chance that the man I was about to meet had had a hand in Clare's death. At the very least, his behaviour afterwards, including not attending Clare's funeral, was questionable. I intended asking him outright about this, but I wasn't thrilled by that rather awkward prospect – experience had taught me it was unlikely to go well.

I was also aware that as a prominent and experienced traditional healer, Mbekaphezulu was almost certainly in possession of all kinds of powerful muti, some of which I had no doubt he could use to wish me ill if he took umbrage at my questions.

After about ten minutes of driving aimlessly, I stopped beside a sinewy middle-aged man with a pockmarked face, who was digging a ditch outside a small church. Just as Mandla had predicted, the man knew of Mbekaphezulu and gave directions to Zimbili, pointing back down the dirt road. When we finally spotted the healer's home, half hidden among a clump of palm trees down a narrow sand track away to our left, it became clearer why everyone in the vicinity might know precisely where to find him. In an area where almost all dwellings were basic single-storey structures, Mbekaphezulu lived in a vast four-storey concrete compound. The hulking building was ringed by luxuriant fruit trees and old vehicles in various states of disrepair. Its towering facades were hollow and clearly still under construction, punctuated by empty window frames and exposed iron rods.

I drove to the back of the house and parked. An old woman with rheumy eyes was slouched on a plastic chair on a small, shaded stoep, watching us impassively as we got out of the car and walked over.

Sam and I smiled as Zimbili introduced us and explained why we were there. At the mention of Clare's name, the old woman raised her hands towards the sky and thanked God over and over, tears streaming down her deep smile lines. 'It has been so many years since I heard someone say that name,' she said finally. 'My heart sings to hear it.'

The woman told us that her name was Doreen and that she was Mbekaphezulu's wife. She was dressed in a thick red V-neck jersey and a doek and seemed to be suffering from Parkinson's disease. She said that she had loved Clare like her own kin and still remembered her vividly. 'There was no one kinder than her,' she recalled.

For months after Clare's death, Doreen said, she had frequently called the Empangeni police station for updates on the case, until one day a Zulu officer had told her to stop calling if she valued her life. To Doreen, the officer's tone had suggested he was genuinely concerned for her safety rather than issuing a threat.

A shy young woman appeared from somewhere in the dark recesses of the building, and Doreen told her to find Mbekaphezulu. She then invited us to sit with her on the stoep while we waited. After a moment's silence, she asked me if I knew what had happened to Themba and Puleng. I pulled up Facebook on my phone to show her recent pictures of them. Again, Doreen raised her hands to the sky. 'They are beautiful,' she said.

Doreen told me that she and Mbekaphezulu had had eight children, but that only three were still alive. Three had fallen prey to KwaZulu-Natal's rampant gun violence over the years. Two of these were shot dead during a robbery in Doreen's home in 1999; the other was killed by a jealous ex-boyfriend, who happened to be a police officer. 'I hate the police,' Doreen said, switching to English for the first time in the conversation. Another two of her deceased children had been 'sick'. In these parts, that often meant they were casualties of the HIV epidemic, which was still shrouded in stigma. 'Ay! South Africa!' Doreen said by way of a resigned explanation for the shocking extent of her personal loss, shaking her head and tutting.

Doreen and Mbekaphezulu had subsequently taken in and raised several of their bereaved grandchildren. Some of them still lived in the home, including the shy young woman we'd just seen.

This was certainly not an unusual situation in rural KwaZulu-Natal, where countless families were decimated by violence and illness. In fact, fostering of this sort was normal within many poor and predominantly black families, where ideas of kinship were already broad and fluid. The word 'adoption' was often seen as something more formalised and atypical – something that, in the main, only white people did.

Mbekaphezulu finally joined us on the stoep. A tall man in his late seventies with a soft smile and an unkempt grey beard, he introduced himself in English accented with the unmistakable intonations of the old missionary schools. Just like Doreen, he too began to cry when I mentioned Clare's name. He pointed to a lemon tree that he said Clare had planted in his garden shortly before she died. Its branches hung heavy with yellow fruit. 'We were so lucky to have Clare,' he said. 'She was wonderful. I am proud of what we tried to achieve together.'

I asked him about the rumours that he was involved in her death. He claimed that these stemmed in part from his and Jabulani's leaving on a trip to Cape Town to take an agricultural training course a couple of days after Clare's disappearance. Mbekaphezulu believed that the police used this fact to imply that he and Jabulani had known what was about to transpire and had promptly skipped town to remove themselves from suspicion. He added that Clare had arranged the course for the two men just prior to her death.

I had always considered myself a pretty good judge of character and, as was the case with Mcabango, I felt a near-instant fondness for Mbekaphezulu and wanted to believe him. I was also aware of the TRC investigation's conclusion that Clare's death was not an inside job, although that theory was never unequivocally disproved. But once again, I was reminded of how slippery the truth often was in KwaZulu-Natal. How much of it remained buried beneath the surface, and how few men had escaped that period without any blood on their hands. It always seemed that so many of us on the outside looking in had a basic reflex to categorise people according to the binaries of good and bad. But KwaZulu-Natal seemed to repeatedly highlight the fallacy of any such categorisation.

Mbekaphezulu was adamant that Clare's death had had nothing to do with any disagreement within the cattle co-operative. He shared Mandla's belief that the blame lay at the feet of the security police and the IFP. 'Clare insisted that we didn't talk about politics at the cattle project, but of course we knew that some people were IFP members,' he said. 'It is highly likely that there were also informers among our ranks.'

As Doreen had been warned off inquiring into Clare's death, so Mbekaphezulu claimed that he and Jabulani had been told by the police at Empangeni to stop digging into the matter. On another occasion, shortly after her disappearance, he said he was tailed by police all the way from Durban to Manguzi. Whatever the truth, it was easy to see how the rumours about Mbekaphezulu and Jabulani had helped to destabilise the cattle co-operative. The counter-allegations that certain IFP leaders were involved had had a similar effect, promptly undoing much of the fragile trust and non-partisanship that Clare had sought to foster and had bound the co-operative together.

But according to Mbekaphezulu, the cause of the cattle project's eventual collapse in early 2005 was much more prosaic: 'There were no funds left,' he said with a resigned shrug.

From Mbekaphezulu's house, we carried on down another dirt road towards Clare's old homestead, which sat on a hillside above a small stream just a short drive away. Mbekaphezulu had volunteered to show us the way. On his instruction, we stopped the car on a grass verge beneath a row of large mango trees. 'It's up there,' he said, pointing into the undergrowth to our left. But the homestead remained invisible from the road, so Sam and I got out to take a closer look.

I'd seen photos that Clare took of the property in the early 1990s, one of which showed a young, smiling Themba standing on the stoep beneath a thatched awning. The photo had been taken from the bottom of a neat grass lawn in front of the stoep, where dappled sunlight had shone through the branches of a large fig tree next to the house.

I brought up the photograph on my phone as we pushed through the bushes, my arms getting scratched by thorns. I soon located the fig tree, but the structures themselves were in ruins. The dense vegetation was interspersed with piles of rubble but had otherwise reclaimed the homestead's foundations. A recent fire had scorched the ground around the ruins and had blackened or felled many of the surrounding trees. An empty door frame was the only piece of the house still standing. Soon, I thought, there would be no trace of Clare's life left here.

When we walked back down the hill, I found Mbekaphezulu plucking a ripe granadilla from a vine by the side of the road. 'The earth here is rich. It has so much potential,' he said, turning the granadilla over in his hand as he climbed into the passenger seat of the car. 'Clare understood that.'

As we drove back to Mbekaphezulu's property, he told me about the ongoing construction of his house, which had begun in the late 1980s, not long after he'd started practising traditional medicine. He added that the house was built from locally sourced materials. 'I have everything I need here,' he said.

One day, he intended the property to serve as a hundred-room hotel for black clients travelling between Manguzi and Durban or other major provincial urban hubs for business purposes. 'This area has certainly changed a lot,' he said, 'but I could always see the potential, even back in those days when I first started building this place. So whenever I had a bit of money to spare, I would make a few more bricks, and add a little more to the structure, bit by bit.'

At the current rate of construction, it was hard to see the project being anywhere near complete in Mbekaphezulu's lifetime. But rather than folly, I preferred to see an irrepressible optimism in the never-ending venture. It struck me that Mbekaphezulu's incomplete shell of a house was in some way emblematic of South Africa: the vast potential and grand ambitions starkly apparent, but unfulfilled.

We dropped Mbekaphezulu off at his house. Doreen had not moved from her chair and she waved to us, smiling broadly. At least she seemed to have taken some joy from our visit. This wasn't often the case.

Mbekaphezulu wished us well and walked towards his house, before spinning round again, another memory having obviously struck him. 'You know,' he said, 'I make all sorts of muti here in my home. I know all of the plants and herbs around here. I often advised Clare to use muti to protect herself. The day before she disappeared, she finally came to me and told me that she had had a bad dream and asked if I could give her some. But then, she was gone.'

CHAPTER 17

The officer

The small town of Jozini is a two-hour drive from Manguzi, along an undulating road that cuts through a series of dilapidated and water-scarce rural settlements along the edge of the Lebombo Mountains and the Eswatini border. Most of the town occupies a rocky hillside, surrounded by fever trees, above the striking Pongolapoort Dam, whose towering hundred-metre-high dam wall serves as the main road in and out and draws the occasional disconsolate suicide jumper.

Established in the 1960s to accommodate the roughly 900 black workers who built the dam, Jozini experienced a heyday of sorts in the 1980s, when it was both an important outpost in the commercial farming industry and a key strategic node for the National Party's nefarious security operations. In the latter case, the town was useful because it was situated along a popular route for exiles skipping the country into Swaziland. It was also on the route that MK cadres used when they returned home to continue their underground activities, particularly in Durban.

Testimonies at the TRC highlighted the reign of terror, including a string of political murders and abductions, brought about by the Jozini-based officers of the Special Branch, most of whom were trained under Eugene de Kock at Vlakplaas. In Jozini, these officers were known to sometimes dispose of bodies by dropping them into the middle of the dam, under cover of darkness, and then blowing them up with explosives.

Today, the far-flung Jozini is more commonly associated with excellent tiger fishing, terrible service-delivery, or cross-border car-theft syndicates, depending on who you ask. Its past has largely been papered over, amid the persisting culture of silence. After the 1994 political transition, most former members of the local apartheid security apparatus either emigrated to Europe, drifted into peaceful anonymity on secluded sugar-cane farms, or made a seamless transition into the burgeoning and highly militarised antipoaching industry on nearby private game reserves.

As far as I could gather, Lappies Labuschagne was the only one who had stuck it out in Jozini all this time. Although his name wasn't on Gail Wannenburg's list of suspects in Clare's killing, I hoped he would know or have worked with some of the officers who were, particularly the elusive Aubrey Mngadi. I hoped some good old-fashioned door-stepping would encourage him to talk to me.

So, having been unable to get hold of Lappies' contact details, I'd come to Jozini in the hope of tracking him down. I didn't have an address, but assumed that a long-term resident and former cop with a name like his wouldn't be hard to find in a small and overwhelmingly black town.

My first stop was the Jozini Tiger Lodge and Spa, an incongruously lavish spot popular with tourists and the town's handful of well-heeled residents. Its expansive sundeck and infinity pool boasted stunning views across the dam. The lodge had been opened in a public–private partnership with local government and traditional authorities in 2010, in a bid to stimulate the local economy in an area with a staggering unemployment rate of well over fifty per cent.

I spoke to a genial receptionist who, despite his best efforts to remain professional, looked perplexed as I fumbled my way through a vague explanation of my reason for being in town. He hadn't heard of Lappies. He called his manager, who hadn't heard of him either, but pointed me in the direction of the local police station and suggested that I ask there. I'd been hoping to avoid this approach. Firstly, I worried that I might arouse unwanted interest in an area rife with police corruption and where it was possible that some officers from the apartheid days might still be in place. I also found police stations in KwaZulu-Natal, most of which were poorly run and chronically under-resourced, profoundly depressing places.

I got back into my car and sat with the engine off for a moment, wondering what I was doing. I wasn't entirely sure what I intended to ask Lappies, or how I was going to play the whole situation.

The best-case scenario was that over the decades he might have developed feelings of remorse and assist me in a small gesture of atonement. Or that it was all so long ago that he simply wouldn't care about the possible implications of speaking about the killing. But I also realised that this was probably naïve, and that I could just as easily be met with a barrage of expletives, threats, or worse still, the barrel of a gun. I'd spent enough time in KwaZulu-Natal to know that a combination of these three alternatives wasn't entirely improbable.

My reluctant visit to the police station would do little to assuage my growing sense of doom. I walked into a typically drab reception area, where an overweight and perspiring Zulu officer listened with an air of palpable and unwavering disinterest to an array of issues presented by crestfallen locals. When my turn came, he waved me through to the offices at the back of the compound before I'd even finished my request, telling me to speak to a Detective Dlamini.

The detective's door was ajar, and he seemed to welcome my intrusion. He spun around to face me in his swivel chair, as if he'd been waiting for my arrival for some time, and asked me to take a seat. A laconic but affable man with deep frown lines,

Dlamini briefly lamented his substantial caseload, which he said was dominated by vehicle thefts and deadly lovers' quarrels, then asked me what he could do to assist me.

Still a little unsure of myself, I stalled for a bit, asking Dlamini about his own history in the area. He told me that before the end of apartheid, he had worked as an underpaid 'garden boy' at the police station. At the time, it was still being used by the state security police. 'I used to see a lot of fishy things around here in those days,' Dlamini said. After the transition, he signed up to be an officer, and became one of the first black detectives in the newly integrated precinct.

A few of the Special Branch officers had hung around for a while, working side by side with the new recruits, although Dlamini implied that the different groups didn't mix much. I asked if Lappies Labuschagne was among the old guard. Dlamini nodded solemnly. 'Miserable racist bastard' was his curt summary of the man.

He told me that he'd also worked with Mngadi, but only briefly. He recalled that Mngadi had made a swift and rather inauspicious departure from the station, though he couldn't remember the precise details and didn't know where he had ended up. He confirmed that Lappies still lived up the road and that he could show me how to get there. He seemed eager to get out of the office for a bit.

We drove for a few kilometres up the steep hill out of town, in the direction of the Eswatini border, until we reached a narrow and unmarked dirt road that veered off to the right behind a rugged hillock. 'You'll find Lappies' house at the end of that road,' Dlamini said, then unexpectedly asked me to turn around and drop him back at the station. 'If I go with you, things might not go well,' he said, by way of a somewhat cryptic explanation. 'He can be a very difficult man.'

I dropped Dlamini off and took his cell-phone number in case of any emergencies, then drove back up the hill and turned onto the dirt road. As my small rental car bumped across the sharp stones and loose gravel, I glanced at my phone and saw the service bars steadily decreasing. I felt a surge of paranoia. It had become an increasingly pervasive sensation over the course of the past year, as I'd absorbed the countless stories of murky and unsolved assassinations across the province. It hung heavy in the air of so many of KwaZulu-Natal's violence-stricken small towns, where it was hard to talk to anyone about such matters without them constantly looking over their shoulder. It was contagious.

I stopped the car before I lost cell reception altogether and dashed off a quick message to a colleague, saying that if he didn't hear from me again within two hours, he should call Detective Dlamini at Jozini Police Station. I attached Dlamini's number and dropped a pin showing my location, and then continued on my way. Fifteen minutes later, I reached the end of the road, where a lone sprawling house perched precariously on the edge of a sheer rock face that fell away to the water's edge, about a hundred metres below. The house had a spectacular vista across the Pongola River gorge. The water shimmered in the bright mid-afternoon sunlight.

I was met at the door by Lappies' wife, a small woman with short, quaffed grey hair and glasses. She showed me into the lounge without asking any questions, then disappeared into the recesses of her home, dragging a huge Bernese mountain dog with her by the collar.

Lappies, who was reposing on a daybed in the corner of the room, sat up with obvious discomfort and a quizzical but not entirely unfriendly look on his sharp-featured, world-weary face. 'Sorry, I've got a terrible back problem,' he said in a thick Afrikaans drawl. 'What can I do you for?'

I gave him an oblique overview of my intentions to write a book about the history of political violence in the area, being careful to avoid any specifics that might raise his hackles. 'I'm not sure how much help I can be,' he said sceptically, but he seemed willing to at least hear me out, so I pulled up a chair and opened my notepad.

Lappies said he was seventy-two, but he looked about a decade older. He had moved to Jozini from the former Transvaal in 1976. At the time, Jozini was still 'a one-horse town' with just four shops, about three hundred white households, and only four police officers stationed here, he said. In his telling, it was a safe, friendly, peaceful community back then. 'Nowadays, people are killing each other every other day, even the politicians,' he said. 'We had a much better South Africa in the old days than what we have now. At the very least, people could get jobs then.'

Lappies claimed he hadn't always felt so jaded about the new South Africa. 'Even after 1994, I still believed I was working for something good,' he told me, though he'd left the police in 1995 due to medical issues. 'I wasn't fit enough to carry on, but I was still sad to leave,' he said. He went on to run a construction company that built Reconstruction and Development Programme (RDP) houses in the area's townships. He had retired recently, as his health had continued to deteriorate.

Lappies' three children were married with their own offspring, and all lived in Europe. He said they were constantly trying to convince him and their mother to emigrate as well. 'But I'm happy here,' he said. 'Why must I run away? For what? I've done nothing wrong.'

He then veered off-topic and began a long and predictable rant about how the racial quota system was destroying rugby, but I could feel that he was slowly warming to me, so I let him chatter on for a while before interrupting to ask if he knew Aubrey Mngadi. 'Yes, we worked together,' Lappies said. 'He was a good, honest guy. We were like a family, all of us colleagues. The black and the white.'

He told me he'd heard that Mngadi had died some years previously, though he didn't know the details. 'Most of my colleagues from those days have passed on,' he said.

With my most promising link to the plot behind Clare's murder now apparently removed from the equation, I felt I no longer had much to lose, so I homed in on more direct questions about Clare. 'Terrible story,' Lappies said, unconvincingly, when I recounted the details of what had happened to her, and the alleged involvement of some of his colleagues. He claimed he had personally never received any intelligence on Clare, though he admitted 'checking out' other ANC members in the area. 'We were defending our country,' he proffered by way of explanation, then added with an ironic smile: 'Now the enemy is our friend.'

Having finally revealed my cards, I sensed a shift in Lappies' demeanour. He vacillated between being cagey and evasive one minute, then overly ingratiating the next. I was sure he knew the art of interrogation inside out, and I sensed that he was beginning to toy with me. So I thanked him for his time and made to leave. He got up from the bed for the first time since I'd arrived, put on some tattered slippers, and followed me out to my car, propping his back up with his clenched right fist and wincing with each step. The enormous dog reappeared at his side as he shuffled along.

When I climbed into the driver's seat and reached out to close the door, Lappies gripped it tightly with his free hand. He suddenly seemed reluctant for me to leave. There was a moment's awkward silence. 'You know, bygones should be bygones,' he said finally, fixing me with a grave stare. 'These old stories should be left alone. It's finished. Let's move on.' Then he let go of the door.

CHAPTER 18

The trail goes cold

Lappies promised me that he would chat to former colleagues who might know something about what had happened to Clare. But after a few evasive replies to my follow-up messages over the next few weeks, he ignored me. Similarly, my calls and messages to IFP member Isaac Ntsele, who had withdrawn his cattle from the co-operative shortly before Clare's death, went unanswered. With the death of Gideon Zulu – a controversial and divisive figure both as a royal prince and as an IFP leader – in 2006, another lead had gone to the grave. He had ordered the boycott of the co-operative, and was said to have instructed his followers to eliminate ANC members who came under the guise of development workers.

Nor did I have better luck with ANC people. Ronnie Kasrils, who Rachel maintained had recruited Clare into MK, denied anything more than a 'vague recollection' of her. This despite both Rachel and a former MK colleague specifically remembering Kasrils meeting Clare at her brother John's house in Harare. According to this colleague, after that meeting, Kasrils had said he personally would be Clare's handler.

In one of the few replies that Kasrils sent to my emails, he forwarded me a brief correspondence he had had about Clare with Bill Anderson, another former senior ANC military intelligence officer, who he said was 'closer to the operatives'.

'I have a vague memory of the two of us meeting her,' Anderson had written to Kasrils. 'I also have a vague memory of someone bringing us some recce photos of the military base at Jozini on the Swazi border. Was that her, and if so there must have been two visits? And asking her for information on the commandos and Security Branch in the Empangeni – Eshowe area. Like you, I generally remember things when prompted. But I am really battling here.'

Kasrils had responded: 'It appears that her family think that I had far more to do with her than was actually the case, but that usually happens when such a person has died. They have presumably mentioned that they "worked for me" and then it is imagined that it was a very close relationship, when as you know there were all kinds of intermediaries between the operative on the ground and us at headquarters.'

I subsequently spoke to Anderson, who now lived in London, over Skype, and he had little more to offer on the subject. Kasrils declined to talk to me over the phone or to meet in person, citing ill health as an excuse. But I couldn't shake the feeling that he was being deliberately prevaricative.

Part of me reasoned that this was hardly unusual behaviour for someone who had spent many years at the forefront of covert operations, where secrecy and smokescreens were crucial parts of the armoury. But there was another part of me that kept thinking about the allegations that had been made by Vusi Pikoli and Anton Ackermann regarding the ANC's intentional squashing of apartheid-era cases and the suggestion that their own members were implicated.

During my reporting in KwaZulu-Natal for other projects, several seasoned local researchers had told me the ANC had plenty of skeletons in its closet concerning events in the province in the final years of apartheid. I also thought about a telephone call I'd had with Clare's friend Peter Rutsch, the Legal Resources

Centre attorney, who had occasionally stayed at her homestead in Thandizwe when doing work on land rights in the area.

Rutsch was pulled in to assist with the inquest into Clare's death in 1995. Shortly afterwards, he was visited by a 'very senior' MK intelligence officer at his home in Durban. 'We sat under a tree in my garden and he interrogated me for about two hours,' Rutsch said. 'He was an enormous guy and quite frankly rather terrifying. He implied that he was working on some kind of investigation and would let me know what the outcome was. But then he disappeared and I never heard anything further from him or from anyone else in MK, though not for lack of trying. I have to say when I look back now, I have the fairly strong impression that this guy was there to find out how much I knew, whether or not I was a threat, and to make me feel a bit intimidated.'

While Rutsch had reiterated that the security police remained the primary target of his suspicion for Clare's death, he echoed Gail Wannenburg's sense that the plot was probably thicker than that, and that many people in Clare's orbit in and around Manguzi knew more than they had let on. 'I'm sure the people there know what happened,' he said. 'It's a close-knit community. In these kinds of rural areas, everyone knows everyone and they know what's going on. But they keep their mouth shut because they're afraid of the consequences if they don't. Even today.'

I was also unable to trace other possible perpetrators from Wannenburg's TRC report, including two more former security police officers with the surnames Nyawo and van der Merwe. As far as I could ascertain, neither Julius (the man who crashed the bakkie) nor the man from out of town known as Hazel Buthelezi (who inquired about Clare the night before her abduction) had ever resurfaced. Nor was I able to track down Clare's domestic worker, Busisiwe. While some members of the cattle project, including Mbekaphezulu, said they remembered her, none of them had seen or heard about her for some years.

While in Jozini, I found out that the tavern owner who had told Wannenburg he'd seen Mngadi drive past with Clare in the car had died a few years previously. His tavern was now a car-repair shop. Even Wannenburg couldn't provide much further help. We spoke on a couple of occasions over the phone, but she said she was in the early stages of a degenerative brain disease and sometimes her memory was 'patchy'.

I tried more peripheral avenues, too. These included speaking to Ambrose Ndhlovu, a member of the NPA's Missing Persons Task Team. He was in contact with a number of askaris who'd been deployed in KZN. In fact, he and his team frequently depended on them to provide information regarding the hundreds of still-missing apartheid victims. Yet none of them had heard anything about Clare.

I began to wonder if my investigation into her murder had simply run its course, at least for now. Even if I did manage to find and confront more of the suspected perpetrators, it was unlikely that I would extract any kind of confession from them, particularly given the renewed calls for prosecutorial justice for apartheid crimes.

Drawing on all of my reporting thus far, I wrote a three-part feature series on Clare for *New Frame* in January 2020. Titled 'The killing of an unassuming activist', it was published in instalments over a week in mid February. When I was feeling optimistic, I told myself that maybe the series would help to shake something loose with regard to Clare's case. Perhaps someone who knew something would read it and contact me to set the record straight. Deep down, however, I knew this was unlikely.

In truth, I was running out of steam. I was also about to be pulled off on another project for at least a month.

Having had a rather difficult year financially, in addition to feeling jaded about my work in general, I'd been flirting with the idea of other sorts of jobs. After being recommended by a colleague, I'd managed to land a short-term contract as a communications consultant for the World Health Organization, working out of their regional headquarters for Africa in Brazzaville, the capital of the Republic of the Congo.

I was due to fly back to the UK at the beginning of March 2020, to sort out a Congolese visa and attend a good friend's wedding, before flying on to Congo on 15 March. As well as providing an entirely new work experience, I hoped that some time away might also be good for my marriage, which now seemed to be disintegrating at breakneck speed. At the very least, I thought, it would provide a bit of respite from it, and, to some degree, from my life itself.

But there are some things we cannot outrun. On the day I landed in Congo, the country detected its first two Covid-19 cases, and a two-week mandatory quarantine period was instantly imposed. Congo would go into a stringent lockdown and close its borders entirely just a few days later. On my first night, as on many nights thereafter, I paced my small hotel room for hours on end, unable to sit still but with nowhere to go.

The following morning, I heard that a group of visiting Zimbabwean doctors had been rounded up by military police on arrival at the airport and driven in the back of an open pickup truck to a squalid temporary quarantine centre at one of the city's soccer stadiums. Fearful Congolese had lined the streets as the vehicle passed, throwing food and shouting, 'go home Corona!' in an array of languages.

With my head spinning in a blur of irrational panic, I wondered if I was going to end up dead in that place, as the entire world went up in flames.

Two weeks later, as I was about to emerge from quarantine, the WHO headquarters effectively shut down, when some staff tested positive for the virus. Rumour had it that an infectious disease specialist who'd recently arrived from the US had shared a plate of homemade cookies with some of his colleagues during a long Saturday morning crisis meeting, and had inadvertently infected them.

I came to feel a pointed hatred for those cookies, as if it was their fault that I'd flown all the way from South Africa only to end up having to work remotely. For a now-interminable period, the hotel grounds would be my entire, shrunken, lonely world. In addition to my workload for the WHO, I was also supposed to be working on a story for *Al Jazeera* about the lack of justice for ongoing political violence in KwaZulu-Natal. This was to accompany my soon-to-be-released documentary on the same subject. But the issue suddenly felt like it had lost all relevance in the midst of those unnerving early stages of the developing global pandemic.

In fact, for a time, almost everything that had existed in the pre-pandemic context paled into insignificance, not only in the news but also in my mind. I had no desire to contribute to the barrage of stories about Covid-19, but I also couldn't bring myself to write about anything else. Aside from the formulaic press releases and reports I was writing for the WHO, I stopped writing altogether, for the first time in my career.

Meanwhile, back in South Africa, any momentum that had gathered around apartheid-era cases ground to a halt, as the country imposed strict lockdown measures. The case against Joao Rodrigues for the murder of Ahmed Timol had already been delayed for the umpteenth time at the end of February, with no new date scheduled. The Neil Aggett inquest was postponed when the judge was admitted to hospital, and would be postponed again in June 2020, due to ongoing Covid restrictions.

A similar scenario played out in KwaZulu-Natal with regard to more-recent political assassinations. The much-anticipated Sindiso Magaqa murder trial, due to resume after a previous postponement in October 2019, was now pushed back indefinitely. In May, the case of eight hitmen who had allegedly orchestrated a raft of political killings from the notoriously violent Glebelands Hostel was also postponed. It had only resumed in March after various delays, more than two and a half years after the suspects had been arrested.

As the national state of disaster diverted stretched police re-sources towards enforcing lockdown measures, witnesses and whistle-blowers linked to these cases, who lacked adequate state protection at the best of times, now faced a precarious and protracted wait. At the same time, some local activists claimed that provincial political figures were seeking to manipulate the coronavirus outbreak to divert attention away from the rampant corruption that often fuelled political violence.

With local elections slated for 2021, against a backdrop of spiralling unemployment and inequality, it appeared that once again, KwaZulu-Natal was a tinderbox waiting to be set alight.

I eventually managed to get out of Congo at the end of May, two months later than planned. With South Africa's borders closed, I flew instead to the UK. Because of numerous other border closures and the lack of flights, it took me more than a week to get there, via Ghana, Ethiopia and Germany.

I spent the next few months drifting aimlessly between the homes of various friends and family, and avoiding the cities as much as possible. I gradually lost touch with Clare's family. Amid all the uncertainty and upheaval, I found I was struggling to keep contact with most people I knew back in South Africa. By the end of the European summer in September, with still no clear sense of when I might be able to return home and, feeling on the verge of severe depression for the first time in my life, I decided I needed to take back some control of my life. Among other things, I was finally going to knuckle down and write a book.

Having still not written anything or really thought about Clare at all for months, I booked a three-week stay at a writer's retreat in rural France.

At the outset, I didn't know what I was going to write, though I did know that I wanted to practise weaving more of myself into my writing. But whenever anyone else on the retreat asked me about my writing, I found myself being drawn back to Clare's story again and again. Her story was, after all, one of seeking purpose and being true to oneself in an uncertain and often hostile world. It struck me that Clare was an apt hero for our times. Or at least for mine.

CHAPTER 19

New world

My enforced exile finally came to an end in early November 2020, more than eight months after I'd left South Africa bound for the Congo. As the plane touched down in Cape Town, I felt anxious and discombobulated. So much had changed.

Most significantly, I had recently decided that I was going to separate from Thola and move to France to write a book about Clare. After all those months locked out of South Africa, I was effectively coming back to pack up ten years of my life and say my farewells.

In truth, some part of me had left South Africa a long time before the pandemic struck. I had come to feel, rightly or wrongly, that the only way to get my life back was to distance myself from the country, at least for a while. And this time, it would be on my own terms.

Thola picked me up at the airport. Although we had already been in a trial separation period for some months, I had not yet told her I was leaving. I'd not wanted to break that news over the phone.

She looked happy to see me, and a little timid. I held her tightly and sobbed. To me, the moment felt more like the first step in what would be a long and deeply painful grieving process for the death of our marriage, rather than a happy reunion after so much time apart.

As we drove away from the airport, we were both silent. I guessed that neither of us really knew where to begin. So much had happened. Table Mountain loomed ahead, with a blanket of cloud covering its rugged summit. I felt disconcertingly empty. I had driven that same road 'home', which passes many of the poorest and most overcrowded parts of the city, countless times, but I felt no connection to any of it any more.

Afraid of falling into old patterns and losing my new conviction to keep moving on, I checked in to a bright waterside Airbnb in Marina de Gama for a couple of months, rather than moving back into our Lakeside flat. The next few weeks took on a surprisingly easy rhythm. Between moments of panic-induced activity as I packed up my life, I spent hours in an old kayak exploring every corner of the marina and birdwatching. Most evenings, I sat smoking cigarettes on a rickety bench at the water's edge. Cape Town is a notoriously windy city, but on many of those nights it was so still that the water looked like glass.

On one such night, an otter swam past, barely disturbing the surface as it cut a silent path through the water. Moments after I lost sight of it, a volley of gunfire sounded from nearby Lavender Hill, a regular flashpoint in the Cape's constant gang wars. It was a profoundly South African moment: the striking beauty and vivacity of the country's natural world starkly juxtaposed against its extreme violence and the ever-present proximity of death.

Even after a decade, I hadn't fully wrapped my head around this dissonance. If anything, it had become more and more piercing, until it felt like the incessant wail of white noise. I could no longer stand it. I longed for quiet.

A couple of weeks later, I met with Puleng one morning at Starlings, a quaint cafe with a shaded garden in Claremont. She was sitting at the window with a coffee when I arrived. Given the ongoing pandemic, I was unsure how I should greet her, but she immediately rose and wrapped me in a warm embrace. Puleng seemed much happier and more settled than when I'd seen her last. She told me that she and Jannous, after much scouring, had found and purchased a four-hectare plot of land on a scrubby hillside a little way outside the rural farming town of Caledon, about a two-hour drive from Cape Town.

Within the next year, they planned to terminate their lease on the Rondebosch house and move onto that land. Their intention was to live entirely off-grid, plant an indigenous forest, cultivate their own crops, and keep farm animals for milk, eggs and meat. The creative space Puleng had developed in Rondebosch would be transposed to her new home, where they were planning to set up a recording booth and host retreats.

'If now isn't the time to make some radical changes, then when will be?' Puleng asked after she'd outlined their ambitious plan.

I knew Puleng well enough by now to know that this was not a flippant idea, and that she had inherited a healthy dose of Clare's stubborn determination. Since buying the land, Puleng and her family had spent most weekends, come rain, wind, or shine, clearing brush, digging a reservoir, and beginning to construct an outdoor kitchen. She and Jannous had enrolled in a course on how to build a house from sustainable materials.

'I feel kind of bad, because I spent so many of the early years of my relationship with Jannous encouraging him to unlearn all of this normative masculine stuff, and now I've basically turned around and asked him to be this stereotypical manly man working the land and building stuff,' she said with some glee. The process had also made Puleng think more about Clare and her own determination to go against the grain. She said she wondered if Clare had ever felt fearful, as Puleng conceded she sometimes did as she worked towards a new way of life, a different way of being in the world.

Puleng also pondered to what extend Clare had felt torn between doing what she believed was right and what was best for her children. From my own removed perspective, in an immoral and unjust society such as the one Clare had lived in, I wondered if those were not, in fact, distinct or conflicting considerations. In many ways, could the same not be said of our contemporary context?

After almost an hour of catching up, I told Puleng about my resolve to knuckle down and write a book about Clare. It was daunting speaking it into being. I'd only recently made the decision, and this at a time when so much else was happening in my life. Actually, I had thought very little about Clare over the past eight months, though she had been present somewhere in the background. I was also afraid of feeling bound to South Africa as I set out to build a new life elsewhere. To some extent, after all, I was emigrating to extricate myself from the residual trauma I believed I'd accumulated from my decade-long experience of the country and its manifold injustices.

But there was another element of me that knew I could never entirely leave South Africa behind, wherever I went. The country was a part of me now, as it had been a part of Clare even during all those years of familial exile.

As conflicted as my feelings about South Africa were, and as much as I, again like Clare, often felt a perpetual outsider, I had not felt such a sense of belonging anywhere else. Even England, my native land, was increasingly alien to me these days.

I could also not deny that I had had an influence on Themba and Puleng, and vice versa. Whether it was serendipity or otherwise, I'd walked into their lives at a time when they were beginning to revisit the memory of their mother and had added fuel to that slow-burning fire. I'd also felt drawn to them both to an extent that I'd not expected. It was a feeling I still struggled to understand, which made it both anxiety-inducing and simultaneously alluring to my inquisitive nature. I wanted to know what it meant.

I told Puleng that I was planning to do another KwaZulu-Natal trip, to get a better sense not only of Clare's life in Manguzi, but also of some of the other places that had formed an integral part of her life. I asked her if she would join me.

'You know, it's so strange, I think for a while after we spoke about it last time, I actually realised that I wasn't ready to go back there, both emotionally and physically,' Puleng said. 'But then just the other day, I was thinking that now really is the time to do it. I also really need to get over my innate fear of rural South Africa, and I think KZN is precisely where that needs to happen. So all of this has been going around in my head, then you show up again right on cue. Just tell me when and I will be there.'

A few days later, I messaged Rachel to see if we could meet. We hadn't been in contact since a brief WhatsApp correspondence at the beginning of March, just days before I left the country and most of the world went into lockdown. 'I had wondered where you were,' she wrote back.

We met on a Wednesday morning at her Claremont house. As soon as I arrived, I sensed that she had decided to let her guard down with me. My articles about Clare for *New Frame* had convinced her that she could trust me to do justice to Clare's story. Puleng also told me that she had been putting in good words for me.

This growing trust brought with it its own kind of pressure. The more open Clare's family became with me, the more time they invested, the more intimate details they were willing to disclose, the greater the burden of responsibility I felt. I had never been so deeply intertwined with anyone I'd written about before.

We caught up over coffee in Rachel's conservatory as Lis, a deputy vice-chancellor at the University of Cape Town, joined her umpteenth Zoom meeting in the office, and Asterix and Trotsky ran around in the garden. Like Puleng, Rachel seemed noticeably happier and more settled, although she said that things between the two of them had been somewhat strained in recent months, in part as a result of Covid. In Rachel's estimation, Puleng was falling victim to some of the abundant conspiracy theories and misinformation around vaccines. 'We've been fighting a bit about it,' she said.

Across Africa, recent history showed that not blindly trusting what the government or large international organisations told you was not an altogether unreasonable position. It seemed to me that it was easier for the South African government to blame ignorance and misinformation for vaccine hesitancy rather than acknowledging their own role in the steady erosion of public trust, in particular since the start of Jacob Zuma's tenure as president in 2009. But it also struck me that some of the frequently vitriolic divisions around Covid-19, which had afflicted so many families I knew, including my own, often mirrored wider ideological ruptures between different generations. In South Africa, I saw it in the way that, say, Mandela's legacy was now being debated. Many young people referred to him as a 'sell-out'. Or in the way that white liberalism was being picked apart. Or in conversations about white privilege, cultural appropriation, intersectionality and so on.

I sometimes wondered how Clare's story and the way she'd chosen to live her life might be perceived in today's contested climate. And to some degree, how I, too, would be perceived for having centred my book on the story of a white woman. There were, of course, so many other stories I could have chosen. But to constantly pick apart our choices could easily become debilitating. The fact was, that this was the path I was now on, and I intended to follow it to its end.

As the December festive season approached, the second or, in some cases, third waves of Covid were sweeping most of the globe. A new and more contagious strain had emerged in the UK. Shortly afterwards, another similar variant was detected in South Africa. A number of European countries talked about imposing travel bans on both the UK and South Africa. Some did and then promptly reversed them. With growing rumours of further lockdowns imminent in South Africa and France, and with the deadline of the Brexit transition period (1 January 2021) also fast approaching, I decided to move my return flight forward a month, and slipped back into France at the end of December 2020. I hadn't even got around to telling some of my friends that I was leaving. On New Year's Eve, I received a message from a good friend wishing me and my wife all the best for 2021.

Bizarrely, I welcomed in the new year by breaking an 8 pm curfew and dancing to Toto's 'Africa' on a cobbled village street overlooking a medieval abbey. My companions were two American women I'd met only a few months before but who, in that moment, I felt knew me better than anyone.

For the first time in ten months, I fully unpacked my suitcase, without any prospect or intention of having to repack it for the foreseeable future. I spread my meagre possessions around my new home, an eccentric three-storey cottage with sky-blue window shutters, exposed beams and rough stone walls. My scant wardrobe, small assortment of books and a few random keepsakes certainly weren't enough to make the place feel much like it was mine, but I didn't mind. I had spent long enough trying to build a home in South Africa only to pack most of it into boxes, which were then dumped in the dank attic of my apartment.

Ten years previously, almost to the day, I had set out from Paris for South Africa, only to come full circle now. Back then, I'd left a girlfriend and a handful of friends and, armed with a single suitcase, gone off to start a new life. Gone off with little sense of what I intended to do with my life, and embarrassingly little knowledge about the country I'd chosen as my new base. In hindsight, I'd also known embarrassingly little about myself.

Now I set up a makeshift workspace in the spare room of my new house and began to write – not just about Clare, but about myself, my marriage, my life, my fears. It all poured out. I'd spent so long effectively hiding myself behind, or sometimes inside, other people's stories. I believed that this was part of what had drawn me to Clare: a strong sense that many parts of her story could stand in for parts of mine, or at least serve as a vehicle to secretly explore those parts. But now, there had been an important shift: I no longer felt I could extricate myself from the story.

I wondered if I had deceived myself into thinking that I was not personally involved in previous projects, or that I was just some kind of benign cipher. Was the idea of the objective observer ever anything more than a myth? Intentionally or not, I always brought myself to bear on my stories in some way or other. And not just on their contents, but on their subjects, too. I decided, then, that the most truthful way to write about Clare would be to also write about myself.

Over the following six months, I maintained sporadic contact with Puleng and Rachel as I wrote and adjusted to life in France. Themba, meanwhile, seemed to have withdrawn again, and didn't respond to my messages.

Paradoxically, it was easier to write about South Africa from afar. It was as if I could better see the forest because the trees were no longer right in front of me. It also felt a less visceral process, and one that was easier to step away from when I took a break or finished up for the day. I knew, though, there was always going to come a point where I would have to go back. Certain details of the story could only be filled in by being on the ground.

In July, while visiting my ailing father in the UK, I sent Puleng a WhatsApp message asking if she was still keen on a road trip around KwaZulu-Natal, and proposed dates for September. 'I would LOVE TO!' she wrote back.

CHAPTER 20

A homecoming

On 28 September 2021, Puleng and I boarded a Safair flight from Cape Town to Durban. We chatted with a palpably nervous excitement for most of the two-hour journey. When the conversation finally lulled, I read while Puleng fashioned a makeshift doll from a couple of sheets of paper ripped from her journal. She gave this to a disgruntled toddler who'd been giving her mother a hard time in the row in front of us. It worked like a charm. It also made Puleng think about her own children. 'This will be by far the longest I've ever been away from them,' she said to me sadly.

After so much time and anticipation, not to mention a few months of living with the ever-present possibility that the ongoing pandemic might scupper my plans, I could hardly believe the trip was finally happening. In the last few days, I had reworked the itinerary a couple of times to accommodate Rachel and Themba, who'd decided they wanted to join us for some of the trip.

With all of this, the pressure that had been mounting for some time now reached fever pitch. Over the preceding couple of years, I'd come to feel embedded in the lives of Clare's family. That feeling would increase once we were on the road together. This was also the first time I had done any proper field reporting since the pandemic had struck. I'd spent April in Guinea, doing some communications work for the WHO, so I was not entirely rusty, but this was different. This was my own. And I was different, too.

I'd quit smoking for the second time in my adult life about seven months previously, but within minutes of our arrival at our Airbnb in a quiet Durban suburb, I lit up on the balcony with Puleng. We also promptly raided the minibar's selection of craft gins, then later went out for further drinks at Cubaña on Florida Road, one of the main hubs of Durban's nightlife. Without either of us having articulated our need, it was clear that we both had to take the edge off at the outset of our trip.

The next morning, beneath a leaden sky, we set out for the rural town of Melmoth, where Clare had worked in 1981, on Robin van der Plank's farm, before going off to agricultural college in Zimbabwe. Our route followed the coast almost to the town of Empangeni, where we cut inland into the striking, forested hills of the midlands. It was in Empangeni that Clare's bakkie had been found, twelve years after her formative stint on the farm at Melmoth.

Our first stop was at a roadside Wimpy to meet with Francois du Toit. As a Department of Agriculture employee, he had been scheduled to meet with Clare to brand the project's cattle on the morning of her disappearance. We took a booth in the fast-food restaurant, where Puleng and I drank oversized coffees and Francois sipped slowly on an orange juice. He was a shy man with a kind face, long thinning white hair, a ruddy tan and calloused hands. He seemed a little stunned to be meeting an adult Puleng and struggled to hold eye contact with her. 'I brought something for you,' he said, producing an envelope with a couple of old photos of Clare and some of the other members of the cattle project.

In both photos, Clare had her head tilted slightly to the side and one side of her face cupped in her right hand, while her other arm was wrapped around her waist. 'She was always standing like that,' Francois said, smiling. 'It was like she was trying to make herself smaller, to never be the centre of attention. She was a very humble person.'

Francois also recalled Clare bringing Puleng to various meetings with groups of white commercial farmers to whom she hoped to sell cattle. They were soon seduced by the 'very noisy' toddler in the room. Clare's unassuming personality did the rest: 'She was very quiet. She never said much, never made any demands, she'd just ask a few questions and she was always willing to listen and to interact with everyone. That's why she was also accepted by the commercial farmers. These were almost all old, white men, many of them Afrikaners. In those days, it was quite unique for her to be able to do that.'

Francois had no doubt that if Clare had remained alive, the cattle project would have been a success, and an incredibly rare one at that. 'I'd seen so many of these kinds of projects fail,' he said. 'With Clare it worked so well because the community were really involved in every aspect of it. I also think a lot of people come in and don't consider how rural people live, their perspectives – they don't understand them. But Clare did. She took the indigenous knowledge and combined it with science, and that's why it worked so well.'

I asked Francois about his recollections of the morning Clare went missing. As with so many people I'd interviewed about that day, even twenty-eight years later, his memory was sharp and precise. 'When she was late we assumed that maybe she'd had a problem with the bakkie or something, and we just carried on with branding the cattle anyway,' he said. 'But by about 2 pm we started to get worried, and we went to Manguzi Police Station. A black officer told us not to worry and that she'd surely show up sooner or later, but then just as we were leaving, he called us back and told us the bakkie had just been found in Empangeni. That's when we realised that something was surely wrong.'

Francois added that he had 'walked into brick walls' when he tried to find out what had happened to Clare. He also claimed that two of his colleagues at the Department of Agriculture had been arrested and interrogated for hours at Empangeni Police Station when they tried to inquire about Clare. 'That was certainly strange,' he said. 'The police asked them a lot of difficult questions, and it was like they were trying to make them out to be guilty when there was no way they had any motive.'

Francois also told me that he had read my articles for *New Frame* before our meeting, and that he had personally known two of the police officers I had mentioned: Rassie Erasmus, the captain who had assaulted Sipho and who had drawn significant suspicion from Clare's family; and Lappies Labuschagne, the officer I had tracked down in Jozini. Francois' son had attended high school with Lappies' daughter. 'It was a very small community in those days,' Francois said. 'We knew and would interact with all of the policemen, though they were mostly a strange bunch.'

Francois told me that Erasmus had left the police a long time ago and gone on to work as a security consultant for a bank, before he contracted cancer and was forced to retire about five years previously. He'd recently died of Covid-19. 'I attended his funeral just this past weekend,' Francois said. 'I was always sure that the police were involved in Clare's death, and there were a lot of rumours in those days about a particular officer, who I won't name, who had connections to both Vlakplaas and Special Branch. I used to ask Rassie about this sometimes, but he always told me to just forget about it, that I wasn't going to achieve anything.'

Francois described Lappies as similarly cagey. 'He would tell me that Manguzi wasn't his area, so he had no information,' he said. 'But although he was technically just a warrant officer, he was in many ways the main man in the area, because he spoke perfect Zulu and was accepted in the community, so he had a lot of local knowledge.'

I was interested in how Francois, working closely with rural black South Africans on the one hand and rubbing shoulders with apartheid security forces on the other, placed himself in the fraught and riven political spectrum of the time. 'My motto was always that we just talk cattle, we don't talk politics, and I'm the same even today,' he said. Nevertheless, it was clear that he had a keen understanding of the country's inequalities and injustices. He told me he used to have Ingrid Jonker's famous anti-apartheid poem, 'The child who was shot dead by soldiers in Nyanga' (which Nelson Mandela had read at his inauguration in 1994), framed on the wall in his house. In the 2007 translation into English by André Brink and Antjie Krog, the poem reads as follows:

The child is not dead
the child raises his fists against his mother
who screams Africa screams the smell
of freedom and heather
in the locations of the heart under siege

The child raises his fists against his father
in the march of the generations
who scream Africa scream the smell
of justice and blood
in the streets of his armed pride

The child is not dead
neither at Langa nor at Nyanga
nor at Orlando nor at Sharpeville
nor at the police station in Philippi
where he lies with a bullet in his head

The child is the shadow of the soldiers
on guard with guns saracens and batons
the child is present at all meetings and legislations
the child peeps through the windows of houses and into the hearts
of mothers
the child who just wanted to play in the sun at Nyanga is everywhere
the child who became a man treks through all of Africa
the child who became a giant travels through the whole world

Without a pass

Francois recalled Lappies noticing the poem when visiting one day some years back. 'What is this shit?' he'd asked. When Francois explained why he loved the poem and what he took it to mean, Lappies had scoffed and walked out without another word.

As we left Francois and carried on towards Melmoth, the sky darkened and a steady drizzle soon began. Puleng, equal parts sad and angry after our first meeting, was silent for much of the final leg of our day's journey. With an old flip-screen video camera she filmed drive-by shots of Nguni cows and sugar-cane swaying in the wind.

We stopped for a cigarette, and I noticed a text message from Francois on my phone. 'I can see some of Clare's kindness in Puleng's eyes,' it read.

As we neared Melmoth, the road rose steeply into the hills, and a mist so thick that at times I couldn't see more than a few metres in front of the car enveloped us. Now, far from the familiarity of the city, I sensed Puleng tensing up. 'I know I've said this before, but I really am still very afraid of rural South Africa, as much as I might like to pretend otherwise,' she said. 'I'm a complete urbanite. *I really don't know this*,' she added, as we came out of the mist and she gestured towards the expansive farms and sprawling plantations of wattle and gum trees around us. 'It would have been very easy for me to have become a certain kind of Joburg woman,' she said. 'But I'm making a conscious effort to not follow the path of least resistance.'

As we pulled into town, every lamppost was festooned with campaign posters for the forthcoming local elections. The IFP seemed to be the most active party in this regard. 'Trust us' read the party's simple slogan above a smiling picture of Mangosuthu Buthelezi.

It was clear that the town had been badly hit by the unrest that had ripped through KwaZulu-Natal in July. Some shops and services remained boarded up behind their broken glass storefronts, while sections of the main thoroughfare were still blackened from burnt tyres.

We checked in to a place called Mari's Cottage, one of a small handful of accommodations in town. Having been in the car for some hours, we decided to take a walk around the property's expansive avocado plantation. We talked about family and land and pondered whether vervet monkeys ate avos. Tall, spiky aloes stood like sentries on a steep hillside beyond the property's perimeter.

Shortly before dusk, we drove back into town in the rain to buy wood and meat for an evening braai, and to link up with Nomfundo Xolo, another Durban-based colleague I'd enlisted as our interpreter. We braaied beneath a leaking awning as the rain grew heavier. Nomfundo shared stories of the extent of the violence and unrest that had engulfed the province two months previously, which she'd covered for *New Frame*.

After Nomfundo had retired for the evening, Puleng and I lingered for a while, smoking cigarettes and drinking wine. It was clear that she was a little overwhelmed by the day's events, and probably by the thought of how much more was yet to come. She spoke about Jannous and how safe she felt with him, then she turned to me and said, 'I think I need you to tell me that you will keep me safe out here.'

In December 1998, a man named Dumisani Cleopas Dludla – an induna in the Melmoth area – lodged an historic land claim on behalf of five local communities and almost a hundred claimants who had been forcibly removed from local farms in the 1960s. In 2012, frustrated by a resounding and lengthy silence from the Department of Rural Development and Land Reform, the claimants approached the courts. Some 37 000 hectares of the land being claimed belonged to timber companies, and a further 18 000 hectares were privately owned and being utilised for sugarcane, timber, avocado, beef and game farming. The total value of the land was subsequently estimated at about R2,5 billion. In a major breakthrough for the claimants in May 2018, thirty white Melmoth farm owners finally agreed to sell 11 000 hectares of land to the state, for R760 million. The understanding was that this land would then be transferred to the displaced communities.

This was a significant moment in the history of land reform. According to a 2017 government land audit, seventy-two per cent of the country's arable land was still in the hands of white farmers, who accounted for less than ten per cent of the population.

Since the ANC had come to power in 1994, one of its central undertakings was to relieve this disparity. But the spotty efficacy of its efforts had thus far resulted in only a quarter of such land being restored to black farmers, according to the farmers' organisation Agri SA. Even where farms had been transferred to black farmers, including former farm labourers, a lack of government assistance, whether financial or otherwise, had meant that many such farms now lay fallow. Because of woefully slow processing, as many as 4 000 farms bought by the government were yet to even be distributed to new owners. Land activists hoped that the Melmoth claim would buck the usual trend and come to represent a rare victory in the long process of achieving meaningful land restitution. However, having covered land reform in 2019, as the heated debate around expropriation without compensation had neared its zenith, I was sceptical of any such likelihood. For their part, the Melmoth claimants had already been tied up in legal disputes since the 2018 agreement.

The Ingonyama Trust, which controlled more than 2,8 million hectares in KwaZulu-Natal, had thrown a spanner in the works almost immediately. In papers submitted to the Land Claims Court, the trust had claimed that the land could not be given to the displaced communities because they were 'subjects of the king' and the land belonged to the Zulu nation. The claimants retorted that the trust was being opportunistic.

The matter was eventually thrown out by the Land Claims Court, and a subsequent leave to appeal was dismissed by the Constitutional Court in July 2020. But by that stage, the trust had added another two years' delay to an already decades-long process.

Meanwhile, in November 2020, *GroundUp* had reported that tensions were rising within the community. 'The success of the land restitution may be in jeopardy,' the publication wrote.

I was interested in getting a better sense of the current situation and how Robin van der Plank's farm, where Clare had worked, might fit into the equation. I arranged to meet with a couple of members of the Melmoth Farmers Association at the home of a woman called Sally Calitz, the association's secretary.

Sally was an effervescent septuagenarian with a wicked sense of humour. She greeted us at the gate in a sky-blue tracksuit and pink takkies. Her husband, Johan, whose handgun lay casually on a coffee table, promptly presented us with an enormous platter of sandwiches and other finger food as we settled into our seats in the lounge.

Despite their hospitality and their best efforts to explain the current situation in Melmoth, after an hour and a half, I was more confused by the whole situation than I'd been when I arrived. In fact, as far as I could tell, such confusion was itself a major part of the issue. The claimants, former owners, and various trusts and associations who'd taken on mediation and management of the farms, were all being hamstrung by frequent misunderstandings and mistrust about each other's roles and agendas. Nobody quite knew what the future held for the area's farms. Everyone agreed, though, that the government had remained largely absent throughout the whole process.

Although Sally said she was determined that they would 'still find a working solution' to the current stalemate, I couldn't help but feel that the black communities would inevitably lose out in some way.

The sugar-cane industry, the beating heart of Melmoth's farming sector, had already lost twenty-three per cent of its production over the past few years because of drought. The recent unrest, during which a number of sugar-cane fields had been destroyed, was only likely to make matters worse for small-scale black farmers.

Sally also introduced us to a man called Dennis Wagner. He lived down the road and had worked on Robin van der Plank's farm, which had been known as Protest Farm, for many decades.

A slight and mild-mannered coloured man in his late sixties, Dennis had recently retired, and he kindly offered to show us around the farm. Although part of the property had been bought by the paper and packaging company Mondi for wattle and gum plantations, the rest of the farm formed part of the community land claim. It was being managed by the South African Farmers Development Association (SAFDA), which faced allegations of corruption and of being 'tender-oriented' after it had been awarded a slew of lucrative government contracts. In turn, SAFDA contracted a company called Simamisa to manage daily operations and the workforce on the farm. In Clare's day, Protest Farm had encompassed about 6 000 hectares under sugar-cane. Today, that had mostly been replaced by dense columns of avocado trees.

Dennis led us to a row of labourers' quarters a short distance away from the main farmhouse, where he said Clare had lived, sharing with three other female labourers. While a number of the farm's outbuildings now lay in ruins, the quarters were intact, save for broken windowpanes. Lines of laundry swayed in the breeze in front of them. Loud gospel music came from somewhere inside the men's quarters, which boasted a striking view of a large dam and a wattle plantation on the hill beyond it.

Dennis said that the workers, including Clare, used to swim in the dam on hot days. He also remembered that Clare would often sit outside, playing her guitar. 'She was so friendly with everyone. She was just like the rest of us,' he told me. 'Any notion that she was different because she was white was washed away very quickly.'

As we drove back to town, Dennis was clearly feeling nostalgic about revisiting the farm where he'd lived for so many years. 'Robin was a kind man. He looked after us,' he said. 'I still have many happy memories of that time.' However, he did not seem overly optimistic about the farm's future. 'It still seems to be in good working condition for now,' he said, 'but I've heard that some of the other farms are already falling apart, and there seem to be a lot more unemployed people around town who were previously working on the farms, so that's not a good sign. If everyone finds a way to work together, including with the whites, then maybe it'll work out, but I suppose time will tell.'

We rose early the next morning, for what would be one of the longest legs of our trip, cutting further inland until we crossed into the Free State and reached the town of Bethlehem. We were to pay a visit to the last farm where Clare had worked before her move to Manguzi. Family friend Peter Breslin had hired her to manage the farm's dairy herd. Peter, in turn, had been hired by the local Catholic church, which owned the land, to set up a worker-led farming co-operative.

The farm, which we found at the end of a long, muddy dirt road beneath an imposing koppie, was now owned by a man called Gibbon Osler. I'd been in touch with him before our trip, and he'd kindly agreed to meet with us.

Gibbon had owned and lived on a neighbouring farm during Clare's time. He told me that Peter had left abruptly in 1995, after which the church had tried to get the Department of Land Affairs to take on the land. 'But they couldn't get their act together, so I ended up buying it,' Gibbon said as we drank rooibos in his lounge. 'It had previously been my grandfather's farm, but he sold it to the Catholics in 1960. I actually attended the farm school here for a few years, when I was very little.'

I had spoken to Peter Breslin on the phone before our trip, and he had told me that it had become apparent to him that the worker-led co-op was 'never going to work'. 'The farmworkers never really believed in it,' he added. Peter had then got a job at the Department of Land Affairs and moved to Bloemfontein, where he'd since retired.

Gibbon could remember Clare, though he said he hadn't known her well. He recalled often seeing her riding out to work in a tractor trailer among the black workers. Gibbon's wife, Penny, also remembered a young Themba coming into the small general dealer that she ran at the time.

Before we headed back into Bethlehem to find our accommodation for the night, Gibbon showed us the cottage where Clare had lived during her time on the farm – a low brick bungalow with a corrugated-iron roof. The cottage was at the end of a row of similar structures and looked across an open plain to a high and striking sandstone plateau. 'My mother certainly managed to find some beautiful places to live,' Puleng said as we marvelled at the view.

We drove back into town as dusk descended and went to the Park Hotel for dinner, on the recommendation of our Airbnb host. Built in the 1920s, the building had maintained its distinctly Victorian feel, with thick carpets, a velvet-rimmed bar and lots of wood panelling. As Puleng and I walked inside and looked for a table, the all-white clientele descended into sudden silence, and I felt eyes on us. I noticed a look, not so much of unease, but more of fatigue flash across Puleng's face, and I asked her if she would prefer to go somewhere else. 'It's fine,' she said. 'This has been my whole life.'

To me, we'd just experienced a small taste of the flagrant racism and sense of exclusion that Clare had encountered here with Themba, and which had been at least part of her reason for leaving and moving to Manguzi. Little seemed to have changed in so many farming towns like this, even all these years later.

We ordered enormous meat dishes and beers and tried to talk about lighter things, then drove back to our accommodation and smoked a last cigarette on the stoep before bed. It was only 10 pm, but the suburban street was eerily quiet. Puleng looked up at the clear night sky and sighed. 'You know,' she said, 'this trip is already making me feel that I can be braver in my life.'

The next day was Clare's birthday. She would have been sixty-two. As we drove the long road back to Durban, I wondered what Clare would have made of the rest of her life had she had the chance. I tried to imagine what she might have thought of someone writing a book about her. From what I knew of her, I imagined she would have found it rather strange and uncomfortable, and probably unwarranted.

We picked Rachel up at King Shaka International Airport, outside Durban, and had lunch at a no-frills Indian seafood restaurant overlooking the ocean in Tongaat. Rachel was chattier and more animated than I'd ever seen her, but there was also an anxious energy about her. Puleng was a little more subdued than usual. Her relationship with Rachel had often been 'antagonistic', in Puleng's words, and I suspected they were both nervous about travelling together for a few days.

After lunch, we made our way to Marianhill Monastery. Built by Trappist monks in the late nineteenth century, on a sprawling hilltop about twenty kilometres inland from Durban, its red-brick buildings, interspersed by manicured gardens and bisected by tree-lined avenues, were imposing. I'd last been there with Sam, in 2019. Just before dusk, she and I had walked through an old metal gate near the monastery into a small cemetery enclosed by a stone wall, where we'd searched for Clare's headstone. I'd always felt strangely drawn to graveyards. I liked to wander around them and imagine the different lives and the historical eras that had shaped and ended those lives as I perused the headstones.

In the cemetery, some of the older graves were covered by long grass and vibrant yellow African daisies. Others were so moss-covered or corroded that the inscriptions were illegible. One section was set aside for Catholic soldiers who'd died during the Anglo-Boer War of 1899–1902. Here was yet another reminder that violence was part of the region's DNA. That day with Sam, the only other person in the cemetery was an old woman who sat motionless beside a modest metal cross in the shadow of a large umkhulu tree, as if she'd always been there. The whole place felt trapped in the past.

It turned out that Sam and I had looked for Clare in the wrong cemetery. Now Rachel directed us down a narrow, unmarked road that led away from the main monastery grounds, through tall grass, before turning sharply onto a dirt track that ran along the edge of a second, much larger and more unkempt cemetery. We met Clare's old friend Jane Quin near the entrance, and followed her Bantam bakkie down the track to the far end of the cemetery, where Clare's grave sat beside a tall crucifix, its white paint chipped and flaking.

Unsurprisingly, the grave was a simple affair, with rocks piled around a small headstone and interspersed with clumps of wild dagga and a small bougainvillea tree. 'Beloved mother of Themba & Puleng, dearly loved sister, she lived among and for the people,' the headstone read.

Jane had brought gardening gloves, a trowel, and a garden fork and she, Puleng and Rachel set about clearing the weeds from Clare's grave. I took pictures of the headstone and of the surroundings, but I soon felt awkward watching everyone else working, so I put on a spare gardening glove and joined in.

As I did so, I was struck by the symbolism of the act: just as I was seeking to do in writing about Clare, I was now literally clearing the weeds from her memory, helping to ensure that it was kempt and clearly visible. It was also clearer than ever that I was not some neutral observer in the story. As the dirt from Clare's grave accumulated beneath the fingernails of my ungloved hand and my knees began to ache from squatting, I realised I had become a very active participant.

Once the grave was clear, Puleng placed a small bundle of impepho on one of the rocks and lit it. She sat cross-legged, with a hand resting lightly on the headstone, as she watched its slow burn. When she stood again, I could see tears in the corner of her eyes. Rachel put her arms around Puleng's waist and rested her chin on her shoulder, and they stayed like that in silence for a few moments. Then Puleng wandered off to have a moment alone at the cemetery's perimeter, which overlooked a sprawling informal settlement.

'The cemetery has certainly grown a lot since I was last here, in 2018,' said Rachel. 'None of that section was here before.' She pointed towards where Puleng stood. 'Clare has a lot of new neighbours now.'

As the rain set in again, we drove back to Jane's house in Pieter-maritzburg. It was an uncharacteristically cold evening for the time of year, and Jane lit a fire in the lounge as she and Rachel chatted and Puleng and I stepped outside for a smoke.

For weeks I'd tried to have a phone conversation with Jane about Clare, without success. She'd said she was overrun with work, and while I was sure this was true, I suspected that she was also reluctant to talk to me. But now she shared memories of Clare in fast, fragmented bursts. As with many other friends and family members, she remembered the days immediately after Clare's disappearance in vivid detail. She recalled Puleng staying with her in Shongweni, after Laura Campbell had driven her down from Manguzi. 'I remember the first day we went to the shops, and everything was fine and you were playing happily and so on,' Jane said to Puleng. 'Then I put you to bed and I was patting you to sleep, and you were lying on your tummy and you let out this cry. A primal cry. It was the same as how Clare had described her cry when the rapists were at her door – she used that word: primal. It felt to me like you were letting go, acknowledging, and it having to do with you finally being in a safe place to do so. It was at that moment that I felt like I knew Clare was dead.'

The pain of this memory was obviously still raw for Jane, whose voice began to waver as she recounted it. Puleng, too, looked to be on the point of tears as she listened. But then the mood quickly shifted as Jane returned to happier memories of an intimate friendship that she said was often characterised by 'hysterical laughter'.

The bond between the two women had been strengthened by their experience as single mothers of mixed-race children. 'In those days, we were always viewed as a bit suspect, as if our situation was a reflection of bad life choices,' Jane said. 'It's true that neither of us were very good with the men in our lives. I kept mine around a little longer than Clare did, but that certainly didn't mean any greater success.'

However, Jane maintained this had never really hindered Clare. 'She was fucking balanced,' she said. 'She was just such a solid, solid person.'

'I think she sometimes worried that she wasn't good enough and so on,' added Rachel, 'but at the same time, she was always very stubbornly herself.'

'Ja, absolutely,' Jane replied, 'but she held it so quietly.'

CHAPTER 21

An opening

Having left Rachel at Jane's house overnight, Puleng and I had a much-needed lie-in the following morning, before picking up Rachel again at a truck stop roughly halfway between Durban and Pietermaritzburg. It was a Sunday, and Puleng had made plans to meet with her half-brother Thembalethu at the upmarket Butlers Restaurant in Hillcrest. Via SMS, Thembalethu told her that Sithembiso, another of Sipho's children from another mother, would be joining us.

Puleng was nervous. She also wondered if it was telling that Thembalethu had chosen a restaurant for the meeting, rather than his home. 'Does he think that I'm too white to go to wherever he stays?' she wondered.

As we neared the restaurant, she asked if Rachel and I could make ourselves scarce and leave her to meet her half-brothers alone, then promptly changed her mind and asked us to stay with her. We sat at a table near the entrance and expectantly stared out the window at the car park.

As soon as Thembalethu and Sithembiso arrived, Puleng's nerves dissipated. 'I've never been so excited to meet someone,' said Sithembiso with a broad smile, before wrapping Puleng in a strong embrace.

As they all sat down at the table, no one really knew quite where to begin, but everyone was beaming. There seemed to be an instant bond between Puleng and her half-brothers. But it was also uncanny how different all three of them were from one another. Sithembiso was a rotund and gregarious man with a round face and small features. Thembalethu was broad-shouldered and handsome, with strong features and a much quieter character.

He recalled going to Manguzi with Sipho to visit Clare shortly after Puleng was born. 'I remember it very well. I was very excited,' he said. 'I also remember Themba. He was *very* naughty.' Thembalethu then recounted how Sipho, who he said 'was basically living in hiding for most of my childhood', would often rely on Clare to clandestinely transport him to different parts of the province for secret political meetings or workers' strikes. 'Clare was a very, very brave person,' he said.

Given Sipho's precarious position and frequent absences, Thembalethu had mostly been raised by Sipho's mother. She'd had a staggering fourteen children, seven of whom had since died.

Thembalethu and Sithembiso, who were forty-six and forty-one years old respectively, were both married. Thembalethu had seven children and Sithembiso four, including what Sithembiso jokingly called one 'side baby' each. 'That's Sipho's influence,' he added with a sly chuckle.

Thembalethu worked as an officer for the Department of Correctional Services, which he said could be 'a very dangerous job'. But he also said all the years working in prisons had given him a better sense of what Sipho had experienced at the hands of the apartheid police. 'It really angered me,' he said.

It became clear that both Thembalethu and Sithembiso felt embittered about the way Sipho had been treated by his own party after the political transition, and that this had led to a certain disillusionment with the post-apartheid political dispensation. 'I think that Sipho's party really deserted him,' Thembalethu said. 'He was blamed for bringing arms into the country and pushed aside. He never really got the recognition he deserved for being part of the struggle. Even people like Jacob Zuma used to stay at our home. But they all forgot about him. Before Sipho died, one of the last things he told me was to never get involved in politics. I think he was right. When you look around now, you see that things haven't really changed, despite all that people like him tried to do.'

It was out of a sense of despondency that Thembalethu had eventually tried to find Puleng. 'There came a time when I realised that I was going down the wrong path in my life, and things just didn't seem to be working out the way they were supposed to,' he said. 'I kept thinking about this thing my father had asked me to do [find Puleng]. I recognised you immediately when I finally found you on Facebook,' he added, looking at Puleng.

As the conversation wore on, I stopped taking notes and asking questions and simply observed the beautiful scene of the three half-siblings getting to know each other. The restaurant had emptied out and it was now time for us to pick up Themba, who was flying in from Cape Town. But no one wanted to leave.

When we eventually said our goodbyes, Puleng promised to come back and visit with her children. 'Their family just got a whole lot bigger,' she said.

The next morning, we drove from Durban along the undulating and truck-laden N3 to Hilton, a quaint rural town that was also home to a number of South Africa's most prestigious boarding schools. I'd arranged to meet Creina Alcock at her son Rauri's house on the edge of town.

More than thirty-five years after her husband Neil was killed, Creina, nearing eighty, still lived in a simple thatched and mud-brick homestead on the banks of the Tugela River. In one of her long WhatsApp messages to me, Creina mentioned that she'd now been living on the farm for forty-seven years. (Her missives always possessed a rich epistolary quality that seemed to be from a different era.)

During that time, much of the land had successfully been rehabilitated and ceded back to the local communities. But in other ways, little had changed from the fractious time of Neil's death. In one message, Creina wrote that there was yet another 'war brewing across the river', as opposing clans continued to fight over land.

Our original plan had been to stay with Creina for a couple of nights at Mdukatshani, but on the day that Puleng and I set off from Cape Town, she had fallen and broken her hip. Rauri sent pictures of his mother being helicoptered out of the valley to be taken to the nearest hospital, in Hilton. She was now recuperating for the next few weeks at her son's house.

Having last seen Puleng and Themba as children, Creina was visibly overwhelmed when we walked into Rauri's lounge, where she was ensconced on the sofa in a dressing gown, with a blanket over her legs. Creina was a striking woman with a thick head of wavy grey hair, a broad nose, a long oval face and intelligent slate-coloured eyes. Puleng and Themba sat cross-legged on the floor in front of her as she took in their faces. 'It's been such a long time,' she said with a heavy sigh.

Since I'd contacted her a few weeks previously, Creina had meticulously assembled a large folder of documents to assist me with my research. It contained everything from letters written to the Stewart family and the police after Clare's death to an extensive history of Mdukatshani, written shortly after Neil's death.

She proceeded to rattle off often-disparate fragments of memory and information at such a rate that I struggled to keep up in my note taking. A former journalist herself, Creina was a compelling and lyrical storyteller, weaving excerpts of poems and books into her sprawling monologue. But it also seemed she had been waiting to say these things for a long time, and was now eager to let it all out in one great torrent. Clearly Clare's death haunted Creina. Her memory of the days and weeks immediately after Clare's disappearance was as sharp as if it had happened yesterday.

She recalled that she'd been at the star-studded birthday celebration of author Rian Malan when she heard that Clare's body had been found. The late musician Johnny Clegg, a close friend, had broken the news to her, and then accompanied her outside to get some air as she let it sink in.

Creina remembered going to Johannesburg soon afterwards to help Rachel and Peter look after the kids. 'You were so, so out of it,' she said, looking at Rachel, who nodded in solemn agreement. One day while she was there, Creina recalled Themba writing the word 'Clare' in the dust on the windshield of a friend's car in the driveway.

But even amid the devastating aftermath of Clare's disappearance, Creina held onto some more rousing memories, such as when the white farmers of Zululand had flown their crop-spraying planes over the area to look for any sign of Clare. 'This certainly wasn't something that usually happened,' Creina said. 'It was a sign of just how much she was loved by everyone.'

In the mid-afternoon, we drove to Mdukatshani, where Rauri had arranged a homestay for us with a local Zulu family. We arrived at dusk and were fed hearty plates of pap and chicken, before the men and women were settled for the night in separate rondavels a short walk from each other.

Themba and I smoked a joint beneath the stars and passed the rest of the evening playing cards. Between rounds, I noticed that Themba had mastered various expert techniques for shuffling the deck. 'Clare would shuffle cards when she was nervous,' he said when I asked him how he'd learnt. 'I assume that I picked it up from her. Either way, I've just always been able to do it.'

The next morning, one of the employees from Mdukatshani gave us a tour of the farm. His name was Mandla Makasela and he was a portly, jovial thirty-something man who lived with his parents near the entrance to the property. He took us down to the edge of the Tugela River, where Creina had said her sister Kathy and Clare used to swim. He also showed us another part of the riverbank, where the two young women had sometimes had night-time 'parties' with the local herdboys. Nowadays, a colony of bald ibises nested on the craggy rock face behind their party spot. But as I surveyed the striking, rocky landscapes on either side of the river, studded with cattle and goats, I imagined that not much had changed since Clare had been there, forty years ago.

As we walked back along the riverbank, we crossed paths with a wiry older woman with a scythe across her shoulders. She stopped to greet us in Zulu, introducing herself as Sizana Mbatha. Mandla interpreted as Sizana told us proudly that she had been born there in 1954 and had lived there ever since. Sizana's recollection of Clare seemed vague and possibly conflated with some of the other similarly idealistic young white volunteers who'd descended on Mdukatshani during the 1970s and 1980s. But she told me that there was a local bird whose call sounded distinctly as though it was saying Clare's name over and over, keeping her memory alive.

On the way back to Durban to drop Rachel off for her flight to Cape Town, we took a short detour to Nottingham Road to visit Themba's old school, King's. Google Maps had marked King's as 'permanently closed', and when we arrived at reception, we learnt that the school grounds were now being used as the temporary premises of a new private school called Etham College. As we walked around the campus, much of it was familiar to Themba. 'I'm actually surprised by how much I remember,' he said. Among other things, he recalled spending a lot of time in the sickbay when he'd first arrived, assuaging some of his feelings of loneliness and homesickness by being looked after by the school matron. He also pointed out a patch of grass near the property's perimeter, where he said he 'used to spend ages trying to find four-leaf clovers'.

At the bottom of the campus, beyond a disused cricket field, we walked through a small patch of woodland that to the young Themba had seemed like a vast, unending wilderness. Themba and Puleng linked hands as he led us along a barely visible path, through the dense undergrowth beneath the canopy of trees. On the way back to the car, Themba recalled the fateful day when he was summoned to the principal's office to be told that his mother had gone missing. While Themba remembered Rachel, Peter, John, Jane Quin and Puleng all being there to pick him up and break the news to him, Rachel was adamant that only the three siblings had been there.

Memory is notoriously malleable and unreliable, and I'd noticed that Rachel was sometimes reluctant to accept this when it came to anything to do with Clare. It was as if picking any single piece of her memory apart threatened to unravel her entire remaining sense of her sister. She had already lost Clare once, and I could understand why this might feel threatening to her.

After bluffing our way into a government parking lot, we walked a couple of blocks through the bustling centre of Pietermaritzburg to the white monolith of the Msunduzi Municipal Library, around the corner from the town's City Hall. The library had first opened to the public in 1851, as the Natal Society Library. In June 2005, during a government initiative to rename a number of streets and public edifices in the city, the main library building was renamed in honour of journalist and author Bessie Head, who was born in Pietermaritzburg.

As Themba, Puleng and I walked up the library stairs to the entrance, we saw Head's name emblazoned over the glass doors in bold white letters, beneath the old Pietermaritzburg crest of arms. We were met by Eshara Singh, a former activist who was now responsible for the library's extensive newspaper archives, which occupied two low-ceilinged levels of the building's basement.

Eshara and her staff hauled out copies of the major regional broadsheet newspapers for November 1993. I wanted a sense not only of the media coverage of Clare's abduction on the tenth and the subsequent discovery of her body on the twenty-second, but also of the general news around that time. We sat at a row of desks against the wall and worked our way through a title each. Whenever one of us found something of relevance, we would gather round to read it together, before returning to our respective piles.

As I flicked through the *Daily News*, I was reminded of some of the major global news stories of the time. There were several articles about what would prove to be the first of many allegations of child sexual abuse levelled at iconic pop star Michael Jackson. Princess Diana, who had officially separated from Prince Charles in December 1992 and would announce her plan to retire from public life in December 1993, also dominated the headlines. So too did the grisly murder of Jamie Bulger, a two-year-old from Merseyside in the UK. He had been abducted, tortured and killed by two ten-year-old boys named Robert Thompson and Jon Venables. Closer to home, the newspapers' local coverage was mostly focused on the changes in the political landscape, with a number of headlines heralding the 'dawn of a new era' in the days after the new interim constitution was signed, on 18 November.

A cartoon in the 20 November edition of *The Mercury* showed a baby emerging from the maternity ward on all fours with a tag attached to its nappy reading 'Democracy (?)' and a speech bubble saying 'Hello world!' beneath a caption that read 'Birth notice: To South Africa – after a long and painful delivery ...'. An overarching sense of optimism was interspersed with harrowing stories of the ongoing violence between the IFP and the ANC, but it was striking how rarely this made the front pages. On 18 November, the leading *Daily News* headline heralded the 'Dramatic Nat, ANC deal', with a subhead that read 'Way now paved for April 27 elections.' Among other news items on that day's front page was a 'meowing cat man' who was 'frightening the elderly' and a brief account of 'dops and rock at Cyril's [Ramaphosa] swinging birthday bash.' Meanwhile, a brief story headlined 'Bloodiest October yet', based on a recent report by the Human Rights Commission, suggested as many as 215 people had been killed in KwaZulu and Natal in the past month. This was buried all the way back on page eleven of that day's paper.

Clare's story first appeared in the news on 11 November, the day after she'd disappeared, making it onto page four of *The Mercury* under the headline 'Hunt on for woman seen in bakkie'. Many of the articles in those early days used the same picture that had been glued to the front of Anne Hope's unpublished biography: a smiling Clare in profile, with a young Themba sitting on her lap, his arms raised above his head and looped around the back of Clare's neck. Among various minor errors, many of the papers spelt Themba's name incorrectly, as Tembe.

On 19 November, five days before Clare's body was found, the *Daily News* ran a full-page spread on 'The last steps of Clare Stewart'. Two reporters had travelled to Manguzi in an attempt to retrace her final movements. Then finally, on 26 November, the coverage ended with a front-page *Daily News* article asking, 'Why was Clare Stewart killed?' with the subhead 'Body of community worker discovered'.

The three of us read the article in silence. Puleng let out a deep sigh when she reached the end. Themba photographed the page.

I couldn't help wondering what he might do with that photo. Would he ever look at it again? Over my years as a journalist, I'd seen people take pictures and videos of all kinds of traumatic events. Maybe it was sometimes an instinctive way to establish a feeling of distance between oneself and the event. Or perhaps capturing the moment with even the vague notion that it could then be shared with others helped to diffuse some of the pain, even if any such solidarity ultimately remained imagined.

We hit the road for Manguzi directly from the archives, in the early afternoon. As we left Pietermaritzburg and then Durban behind us, we were soon surrounded once again by vast, rolling expanses of sugar-cane, rippling in the strong breeze. As we neared the town of Hluhluwe, a KwaZulu-Natal safari hotspot, the landscape changed to open savanna punctuated by thorny acacias and fever trees. We passed much of this leg of the journey listening and singing along to the Beatles' and Tracy Chapman's greatest hits, and occasionally pointing out wildlife roaming along the fences of the various game reserves.

We arrived in Manguzi at 7 pm. Although most of the town beyond the main thoroughfare was shrouded in darkness, as Themba looked at the lit-up shopfronts of major brands like Pep and Steers, he was astounded by how much the town had changed from the rural backwater he remembered. We checked in to Kosi Bay Casitas, on the outskirts of town, and had dinner in the lodge's restaurant, next to the pool. The next day would be the last full day of our trip, and as we drained a couple of beers and chain-smoked cigarettes, I was acutely aware of the increasingly unguarded intimacy that had formed between the three of us.

We even started plotting future road trips, agreeing that next time we should hop across the border into Mozambique. I happily went along with the fantasy, though I knew the spell would soon be broken.

We drove to Mbekaphezulu's house late the next morning. Somehow, his vast complex seemed even more unfinished than when I'd visited two years previously. Parts of it were falling into disrepair, having never been completed in the first place.

When Mbekaphezulu greeted us at the back door, barefoot and dressed in shorts and a threadbare collared shirt, I noticed that he, too, had aged considerably. He invited us into his office, where he sat behind a desk, surrounded by shelves of dust-covered jars and vials containing traditional plants and remedies.

Mbekaphezulu introduced us to a second and much younger wife, called Mukhumalu. They had recently married so that he could train her to be a traditional healer and she could inherit his extensive indigenous knowledge. 'Otherwise, everything will be doomed,' he said fatally.

Mbekaphezulu was too preoccupied with his own legacy to show much interest in Themba and Puleng, and he claimed not to recall various memories he'd shared with me about Clare. Strangely, he also denied ever having told me that Clare had planted the lemon tree in his backyard. As the minutes passed, I grew increasingly puzzled by the interaction, and I wondered if

Mbekaphezulu felt that my repeated visits were a sign that I was suspicious of him and thought he had played some role in Clare's abduction and murder, as some locals alleged.

This sense strengthened when Mbekaphezulu turned to me and asked why I hadn't called Jabulani Tembe, who had faced similar allegations and whose number he had given me on my last visit. It was the way Mbekaphezulu framed his question that took me aback: 'Why don't you trust Jabulani?' he asked, although I had never expressed any such sentiment.

A sinister possibility nagged at the back of my mind: if Mbekaphezulu *had* been involved, perhaps he was unsettled by facing Clare's adult children in the flesh.

The not-so-flattering truth of the whole Jabulani debacle was that I'd simply been exhausted, after days of driving all over the province and conducting long and often depressing interviews at a time when I was already feeling burnt out, and I simply couldn't face another phone call. I'd then misplaced Jabulani's number sometime thereafter.

Mbekaphezulu said he would call Jabulani and see if he could speak to us. 'He's going to come here and meet you now,' Mbekaphezulu said after he hung up.

While we waited, I asked if Puleng and Themba could meet Doreen, who'd been so moved to see pictures of them and by the memory of Clare. Mbekaphezulu led us to a dark lounge at the back of the house, where Doreen sat on the couch, wrapped in blankets, watching soap operas on a large flat-screen television. She smiled with recognition but looked a little surprised to see me again. Then her eyes moved to Themba and Puleng, and her mouth dropped open as she realised who they were. 'Themba? Puleng?' she asked urgently, looking back to me for confirmation, her eyes now wide. I nodded. Doreen let out a loud 'Yoh!' and slapped her thighs with both hands, then began to cry. Themba and Puleng kneeled in front of the sofa and tried to console her gently. 'Now, I can die in peace,' Doreen said, her eyes darting from one of Clare's children to the other.

Jabulani soon arrived. He was an eloquent and charming man, with a round face and a Cheshire-cat smile. He greeted Puleng and Themba with a warm and nostalgic familiarity. 'Your mother was very different to ordinary people,' he told them. 'She gelled with everyone. And she always put others before herself. But she was also very stubborn. If she believed in something, she would not give up until she achieved what she wanted. It is a testament to that same spirit that almost all of the people who were part of the cattle project have gone far.'

With little prompting, Jabulani then launched into his recollections of Clare's disappearance and the immediate aftermath. If Mbekaphezulu had become, at best, a little tired of talking about the whole affair and, at worst, cagey, Jabulani was eager to set the record straight. Among other things, he claimed that both he and Mbekaphezulu had briefly been detained and tortured by Special Branch operatives almost immediately after Clare's abduction, and that they had 'harassed' him for months afterwards. 'After we were detained, people in the project, even some of our own comrades, fingered us for the murder. There was already tension about who held what post, and people who wanted to oust me, so the rumours fed into that and things became very bitter,' he said.

Jabulani, who was an active ANC member at the time, added that two 'MK guys' had sought him out in Manguzi. 'At the beginning, they wanted to kill me, as they were saying that I was the driving force behind the murder,' he said with an incredulous laugh. 'But after they spoke to me and others, they were convinced that I was innocent.'

Jabulani was adamant that the Special Branch were the main culprits behind Clare's murder. He claimed that the day before the abduction, he and Clare had been driving home from work when a certain police officer had passed them in the other direction. 'Clare told me that she hated that guy and that they'd had some kind of fight the day before, but she said she'd tell me all about it the following day. But the next morning she disappeared,' Jabulani said.

In terms of the police's likely motive, Jabulani claimed that Clare had had a more active political agenda than many of her close friends and family believed. 'She came here with a mandate to slowly try to introduce the ANC into the area,' he said. 'It was quite difficult, and certainly very dangerous, so you had to be very clever and very secretive. The IFP felt that the area belonged to them, and no one else must come here. So it was clear the only way the ANC could penetrate the area was through NGOs.'

I was dubious of this claim, which did not appear to have garnered any significant scrutiny in the TRC investigation, and directly contradicted the assertions of many other people who had known Clare well. It also, whether intentionally or not, corroborated the story about the alleged order from Gideon Zulu that ANC members who came under the guise of development workers should be eliminated.

As Jabulani spoke, I felt that other parts of his story were being embellished or exaggerated. Among these were the claim that after Clare's disappearance, Special Branch operatives had followed him and Mbekaphezulu onto a plane from Durban to Cape Town, with the intention of taking them both out when they landed.

To be generous, such anecdotes were perhaps not entirely beyond the realms of possibility, but I couldn't shake the doubt in my gut. When I looked at Puleng, I noticed a similar scepticism written all over her face.

At the same time, I struggled to believe that any of this implied that Jabulani had been involved in Clare's abduction and murder. Above all, it was hard to see what he would have gained as the cattle project gradually fell apart after her demise. A man of his obvious intelligence would surely have seen that coming.

Given the culture of silent obfuscation and secrecy that so often pervaded KwaZulu-Natal, I began to reluctantly accept that we would probably never know the full truth of what had happened.

Just as I had done previously with Sam, on leaving Mbekaphe-zulu's house, which Puleng likened to something out of a Gabriel García Márquez novel, we drove to Clare's former homestead in Thandizwe. It took us a while to find the old foundations in the increasingly dense undergrowth. Even the empty door frame, the only part of the structure standing at my last visit, had since collapsed.

Meanwhile, new breezeblock houses had sprung up all around the ruins, gradually encroaching on the now-unmarked perimeter of Clare's property. A group of small children playing in the yard outside one of the new homes stopped to watch us, as we rustled around in the bushes. Themba eventually got his bearings and began to recreate the layout for us, drawing a visual map from his memory and engraving it onto the much-changed landscape like a palimpsest.

The homestead began to take shape in my mind more viscerally than it had when I'd come here before, with only a photograph for reference. With Themba's guidance, I could see the small rose garden beside the house; the verdant lawn sloping down the hill to the stream where Themba swam; the mango and lychee trees that he climbed. I could see the front gate, with the bakkie parked in the driveway. And I could see Clare on the stoep, playing guitar. It was an idyllic scene. And in this scene, Clare was happy and full of life.

When it was time to go, Themba took a jagged piece of the homestead's front wall, with its distinctive maroon and white pattern, from a pile of rubble and carried it down the hill to the car. I decided to also take a memento, and picked up one of the enormous empty snail shells scattered about the place. I turned it over in my hand, feeling its intricate patterns and contours: it too was a remnant of a life once lived.

Shortly before sunset, we drove down an undulating sandy track towards the edge of Kosi Bay, parking our car next to a row of boats that bobbed lightly in the water and a sign that warned 'Hippos and crocodiles – swim at your own risk'. As we walked along a wooden boardwalk beneath the canopy of a thick dune forest, heavy rain pattered against the leaves and thunder rolled across the water from the hills on the other side of the lake. As we came to the end of our journey, the timing was so apt it was almost as if I'd scripted it. Then it struck me that, as the one who had planned the whole thing, to some extent I had.

When we reached the end of the boardwalk, Puleng placed some impepho inside a snail shell on top of the chunk of masonry that Themba had taken from Clare's homestead and lit it. Then the siblings sat side by side, with their legs dangling over the edge, above the water. Puleng leant into Themba, and he lifted his arm to wrap it around her shoulder as they watched the sun slowly set, a kaleidoscope of orange and pink hues breaking through the gaps in the storm clouds. 'I feel so lucky to have you in my life,' Puleng said to Themba.

For a long time now, I'd been trying to get closer to Clare, to better understand her and her legacy. Despite my best efforts and all that had been shared with me by those who knew her, my sense of her was still blurry and abstract. But as I watched Puleng and Themba, it was finally and blatantly clear to me that, above all, so much of her essence was embodied in them.

I hung back and took pictures, not wanting to infringe on their moment and still somewhat unsure of my role and position in their journey, and in my own for that matter. Then Themba turned to me and said, 'Come sit with us, Chris'. Surprisingly moved by his request, I obliged, and the three of us perched there together, smoking a cigarette in silence in the rain.

As the light faded, we walked back along the boardwalk to the car. Themba and Puleng decided to hide the piece of wall behind a tree. They made a pact that one day they would return to find it with her children. They would show them this place. And they would tell them all about Clare. 'It's strange,' Puleng said, 'because I guess, before, I thought that this trip would be about finding closure, or that it would feel like some kind of ending. But now it feels more like it's the beginning of something. It's actually more like an opening.'

The aftermath

December 2021

By the time the South African local elections rolled around, on 1 November, I'd been back in the south of France for a few weeks, enjoying the last of the warm autumnal sunshine. I followed the unfolding events in South Africa from afar, with a strange sense of detachment, as the political parties reeled out the usual mix of platitudes and populism. In addition, the ANC expressed its 'concern' at the latest spate of political assassinations that had inevitably accompanied the run-up to polling day in KwaZulu-Natal.

The election results marked a resounding failure for the ruling party. For the first time since the political transition, its support dropped below fifty per cent. Overall, it gained just 45.6 per cent of the vote, down from 53.9 per cent in 2016. The increasing disillusionment with the ANC was most apparent in urban areas, with the party's support dropping well below forty per cent in Gauteng's three major economic hubs of Johannesburg, Tshwane and Ekurhuleni. In KwaZulu-Natal, the party lost its majority in Durban, sinking to forty-two per cent of the vote, a twenty-point drop compared to 2011, just two election cycles ago.

After my sobering experience of covering the country's last general elections for *Al Jazeera*, in 2019, these results came as no surprise. Unfortunately, nor did the low turnout figure – the lowest since 1994 – of 45.71 per cent.

It was clearer than ever that many South Africans no longer saw any benefit in taking part in the country's formal democratic processes – a damning indictment of the ANC's myriad failures. But to my mind, the poor turnout also highlighted the lack of imagination on the part of the main opposition parties, which had consistently failed to offer an appealing or inclusive alternative. It was undeniably all rather depressing.

I often wondered how Clare would have felt about the state of her country now. Would she have grown jaded and cynical, as had so many of the progressive white South Africans I'd spoken to over the years? Would she have felt an acute sense of betrayal and disappointment, similar to that expressed by a number of the former ANC freedom fighters I'd interviewed? Or would she have conserved a kernel of hope and found new ways to keep dedicating herself towards the country's betterment? I liked to believe the latter.

There were, after all, countless South African NGOs that sought to do exactly that. These included Lawyers for Human Rights and the Foundation for Human Rights, which fought tirelessly for justice for the victims of apartheid crimes. In late November 2021, the Director of Public Prosecutions made a momentous prosecutorial decision regarding one such case, that of the so-called 'Cosas Four'. The case concerned Eustice Madikela, Ntshingo Mataboge, Fanyana Nhlapo and Zandisile Musi, all of whom were members of the Congress of South African Students.

On 15 February 1982, they were lured by askari Tlhomedi Ephraim Mfalapitsa, with the help of notorious fellow askari Joe Mamasela, to a pumphouse near Krugersdorp that the police had rigged with explosives. The ensuing explosion killed Madikela, Mataboge and Nhlapo, and left Musi severely injured. In addition to charges of murder and kidnapping, for the first time in the country's history, a charge of crimes against humanity was included in the indictment.

But there had also been significant setbacks in other high-profile apartheid-era cases. Perhaps most notable among these was the death of Joao Rodrigues, the security police officer who'd been charged with the murder of Ahmed Timol. Rodrigues had died in his sleep at his home in Pretoria on 6 September, his health having steadily deteriorated since the 2017 Timol inquest. 'He is going to his grave with his secrets about what happened that day in room 1026 at John Vorster Square,' Timol's nephew Imtiaz Cajee told a reporter from the *Pretoria News*, adding that the ANC government should be held accountable.

The death of the last apartheid president, FW de Klerk, on 11 November, at the age of eighty-five after a battle with cancer, elicited a similarly dissatisfied response from many. 'He could have taken an opportunity for over thirty years to meet the families of apartheid victims and share crucial information with them so that as families they could find closure, and some could even say to their loved ones "rest in peace"', Thembi Nkadimeng, Nokuthula Simelane's sister, told *Newzroom Afrika* when the government granted de Klerk a state funeral. This move drew unsurprising controversy, considering de Klerk's largely unrepentant legacy.

'It'll be exactly the same when Buthelezi dies, if he ever dies,' said Puleng of the nonagenarian IFP founder and president emeritus, when we spoke briefly over the phone in early December about de Klerk's death. Barring a few brief text messages, it was the first time she and I had spoken since our KwaZulu-Natal trip, almost two months previously. Shortly after that, Puleng, Themba and Rachel had departed for Mexico to attend the wedding of their cousin Phil, one of Clare's younger sister Alice's children.

This marked Rachel and Puleng's first time travelling internationally together since Puleng was a young teenager. Without the constraints and baggage of their familiar South African context, Puleng said she'd seen a new side of Rachel. 'Did you know, Chris, that my mother can stay up and dance until one in the morning? Could you ever imagine?' Puleng said. 'Left to her own devices, she's a bloody party animal. I mean, there I was, sitting next to this woman who raised me, and she was singing the International, the Communist anthem, in English, then Spanish, then Portuguese. I was like "Who are you, where did you come from, and why do you hide yourself so often?"'

Puleng laughed when I asked if she thought the KwaZulu-Natal trip had in any way shifted the often-trying dynamic between her and Rachel. 'Remember my mother and I are already three decades into our relationship. Things don't just change overnight,' she said. But then after a moment's reflection, she backtracked somewhat: 'Actually no, it's really wonderful that she and I got to do something like that together, and I do think it added different layers to how I see her.'

Since returning from Mexico, Puleng had continued the family move onto their rural plot of land. They'd handed in notice for the house in Rondebosch and were steadily packing up their possessions. Ayanda and Kaello had experienced a 'very emotional goodbye' on their final day at school. 'There is no going back now. I put us in this boat and we're now officially floating downstream,' Puleng said. 'I'm much more nervous about it than I was when it wasn't so close. I think it's scary to make decisive choices in life in general. It's much easier to just wake up where you are and keep going, and sometimes even that is fucking hard.'

Puleng also told me that she was planning another trip to KwaZulu-Natal during the Easter holidays, for her boys to link up with Thembalethu and Sithembiso's children.

Themba, meanwhile, had become typically elusive since we'd all said our goodbyes at the end of the trip. My subsequent occasional check-ins and fact-checking requests via WhatsApp had met with a resounding silence for weeks, until I finally managed to pin him down for a phone call in mid December.

We spoke mostly about his reflections on the trip. 'In 2017 I had a very strong focus on this part of my history, because I was working on *Red Aloes*,' he said, 'and I think the trip reinvigorated a bit of that interest in me again, that desire for reconnection with past life and family. Puleng meeting her half-brothers also made me think more about trying to see my father again before he dies.'

Themba then spoke about his growing desire to leave Cape Town and live overseas for a while, something he'd never done. 'I'm thirty-six now, and if I don't do it soon then I fear it might be too late,' he said.

The next day, after months of my pestering him, Themba sent me photos of various letters and postcards that he had exchanged with Clare while he was away at boarding school in Nottingham Road. On one card that was decorated with glittery, cartoon-like guinea fowls, Clare had written what felt like fitting parting words for whatever either of her children would embark on: 'I hope you learn more songs and read lots of stories. I love you very much, Clare.'

Acknowledgements

My first thanks go to Clare Stewart's family, and in particular Themba, Puleng and Rachel. Despite their varying degrees of initial reticence or guardedness regarding my proposed project, they were open-minded enough to at least hear me out. They subsequently spent many hours graciously and thoughtfully answering my questions and delving into often-painful parts of their history for my benefit. I hope that I have related both Clare's story and theirs as truthfully, wholly and compassionately as possible.

I owe a similar debt of gratitude to Vanda van Speyk and Steve Hulbert, who first shared Clare's story with me. Vanda was also a regular sounding board and source of information and encouragement throughout the process of putting this book together. Along with Thola, their daughter and my ex-wife, they also welcomed me into their family, which was another form of invaluable support for a still rather fresh-off-the-boat immigrant from the UK.

There are scores of other former friends and colleagues of Clare's who related their memories of her with great patience. Creina Alcock and Jane Quin were particularly generous with their time and recollections.

Writing can often be a rather lonely enterprise, so I've always been grateful for my small community of colleagues within the journalism industry, who have helped to make it a little less so along the way. In the case of this book, Sam Reinders, Shaun Swingler, Nomfundo Xolo and Zimbili Vilakazi all kept me company on certain legs of my various reporting trips around

KwaZulu-Natal; Nomfundo and Zimbili also provided invaluable interpreting assistance.

When I was first thinking about putting together a book proposal, Kimon de Greef, Jonathan Ancer and Simone Haysom all provided valuable insights from their experiences of working with the South African publishing industry, which was an unknown beast to me.

Other journalists and writers, including Ziyanda Ngcobo and Jacob Dlamini, have been similarly open-handed with regard to sharing some of their trusted sources.

Much of the initial research and reporting for this book was made possible by a Taco Kuiper investigative grant from Wits Journalism School. The financial support was complemented by the encouragement of veteran editor and journalist Anton Harber, who headed up the grant panel and expressed a keen interest in my subject from the outset.

Monica Laganparsad, the editor of *New Frame*, was then willing to give me the additional support and space necessary to write a three-part feature series, accompanied by Sam Reinders' evocative pictures, from which this book would ultimately grow.

Gill Moodie and Sonwabiso Ngcowa saw promise in this book from my initial proposal, and since Sonwabiso subsequently became my commissioning editor, he has continued to express his belief in the value of this project. He has also helped to make its creation feel like a collaborative process. I am also grateful to a number of his colleagues at NB Publishers for their own various contributions.

As has so often been the case with my writing, my mother, Tessa, was the first to read or be read a number of chapters, and she always provided constructive feedback. She shared this role with my partner, Gigi, whose unwavering emotional support has also seen me through some moments of profound imposter syndrome, not to mention various personal hardships that have coincided with the writing of this book.

The rest of my long-suffering family (my father Tony, my sister Letitia, and my brother Billy) have been loyal readers and followers of my work since my cringeworthy first forays into the world of journalism, almost a decade ago. Their dry humour, which goes hand in hand with a typically British aversion to overly effusive affirmation, has also helped keep me grounded.

And lastly, I am immeasurably thankful to the latest addition to my family, my daughter Colette, who was born within days of my finishing the first draft of the manuscript, their respective gestational periods having almost exactly mirrored each other throughout. Even before she was born, Colette brought a new sense of awe, wonder and purpose to my life. This book is dedicated to her, though it will be many years before she reads it.

About the author

Christopher Clark is a multimedia journalist and documentary filmmaker covering underreported social issues, mainly across southern and central Africa. His writing, films and photography have been commissioned by leading international outlets, including *Al Jazeera*, *The Atlantic*, *BBC*, *The Guardian*, *Harper's*, *Reuters*, *Vice* and *The Washington Post*. He has also done regular work for South African titles, including *GroundUp* and *New Frame*. Christopher currently lives between Cape Town and the south of France. This is his first book.